# Social-Emotional Learning Using Makerspaces and Passion Projects

*Social-Emotional Learning Using Makerspaces and Passion Projects* is chock-full of meaningful projects that educators can use to teach social-emotional skills in grades 3–6.

The projects show students how to create a digital calming room, prototype an inclusive playground, and make recycled cards with paper circuits to spread kindness. They also teach young makers how to focus on self-regulation and self-care, engage in community outreach by helping struggling families, and tell their own stories using podcasting and green screening. In addition, the book provides teachers with helpful strategies for scaffolding passion projects, funding a makerspace, and tips for building community and celebrating diversity.

With the engaging ideas in this book, educators will be able to help their students build direct connections to Social Awareness, Relationship Skills, Responsible Decision-Making, Self-Management, and Self-Awareness (CASEL's SEL Framework).

**Julie Darling** is the Founder of Growing Makerspace, LLC and the Media Specialist at the A2 STEAM school in Ann Arbor, MI. Julie has a Bachelor of Arts in Psychology, teaching certification and a Master of Science in Information, from the University of Michigan. She built a makerspace for kids from the ground up and has taught kids technology and maker activities for over 17 years. You can follow her on her website: https://growingmakerspace.com/.

# Social-Emotional Learning Using Makerspaces and Passion Projects

*Step-by-Step Projects and Resources for Grades 3–6*

Julie Darling

Taylor & Francis Group

NEW YORK AND LONDON

Cover image@shutterstock

First published 2022
by Routledge
605 Third Avenue, New York, NY 10158

and by Routledge
4 Park Square, Milton Park, Abingdon, Oxon, OX14 4RN

*Routledge is an imprint of the Taylor & Francis Group, an informa business*

© 2022 Taylor & Francis

The right of Julie Darling to be identified as author of this work has been asserted by her in accordance with sections 77 and 78 of the Copyright, Designs and Patents Act 1988.

All rights reserved. No part of this book may be reprinted or reproduced or utilised in any form or by any electronic, mechanical, or other means, now known or hereafter invented, including photocopying and recording, or in any information storage or retrieval system, without permission in writing from the publishers.

*Trademark notice*: Product or corporate names may be trademarks or registered trademarks, and are used only for identification and explanation without intent to infringe.

*Library of Congress Cataloging-in-Publication Data*
A catalog record for this title has been requested

ISBN: 978-1-032-14510-5 (hbk)
ISBN: 978-1-64632-219-0 (pbk)
ISBN: 978-1-003-23807-2 (ebk)

DOI: 10.4324/9781003238072

Typeset in Palatino, Futura, and Rockwell
by Apex CoVantage, LLC

# Contents

*Acknowledgments* .................................................. vi
*Introduction: Makerspace in a Nutshell* ........................... vii

1  **Use Cardboard to Build Community** ..................................1

2  **Use Paper to Spread Kindness and Raise Awareness** ...............27

3  **Use Fabric to Help Others in Your Community** ....................50

4  **Share Our Stories and Learn about Others through Audio and Video Production** ..................................................62

5  **Facilitate Passion Projects** .....................................99

6  **Fund and Supply Your Makerspace** ................................120

7  **Management, Trainings, and Volunteers** ..........................132

   *References* ....................................................141
   *Index* .........................................................143

# ■ Acknowledgments

This book has been a labor of love, several years in the making. It started out as a completely different book, maybe one I'll publish another time. The book you're reading right now couldn't exist without the help of a lot of people.

First, Willa and Bree for allowing me to drag them to every maker activity within a 60-mile radius, and for all the experimenting we tried together. Brad for years of support with this and all of my other ideas. Stephanie McCauley and the Prufrock and Routledge teams for making this book so much better than it would've been without you.

Terry Lawrence for the incredible photographs (all the good ones are hers). Sharon Norris and Eileen McCallum, my makerspace partners in crime. Also, Nettie Tiso and the Plano Public Library for giving me permission to use their designs.

The following people let me interview them or otherwise lent their expertise (or equipment) which was invaluable – even if not everything made it into this book: Bob Darling for letting me borrow his fancy camera, Kara Darling for lending me her sewing machine, Lianna and Brandon Ruben for *What Do You Do with an Idea?* Laura Russello, Paul Barrow, Andrea Frey, Bill Van Loo, Paul Straka, Matt Monroe, Rob Ryan-Silva, Steve Teeri, Katie Tilton, Joe Bauer, Jon Van Noord, Mark Lawrence, Paula Lawrence, Cathy Darling, Erica Karmeisool, Micaela Balzar, Rachel Wilson, Sarah Primeau, Jan Chernin, Matt Gibson, Meredith Nickerson, Brian Darling, Kirsten Korff, Sherry Grant, Bianca Humphries, Brian Bricknell, Nate Berens, Kim Phillips-Knope, Jenni Lane, Taryn Gal, Dale Grover, Tom Root, Kyle Vorpahl, Shannon Javis, Kathleen Minelli, Emily Gray, Carrie Ragnes, Jeanie Wilson, and Josh Williams.

I am also grateful for the across-the-board support and encouragement from Monique Uzelac, Anne Fitzpatrick, Chris Timmis, Tammy Reich, Jeff Dagg, Amy Janowitz, Sarah Jardine, Sandy Aldrich, Lisa Pham, Kelly Parachek, Shannon Robertson, Diane Fine, Ben Brose, Jen Brose, Carrie Lewand-Monroe, Leslie Calhoun, Jeff Oleksinski, Kristin Oleksinski, Erin Helmrich, Nancy Moroz, Pam Bennett, and my entire book club. Apologies for anyone I've missed.

# Introduction: Makerspace in a Nutshell

In January 2005, Dale Dougherty took maker culture by storm with his publication of the first issue of *Make* magazine. *Make* was ground breaking because it merged the DIY movement with hackerspaces, something that was eventually (starting in 2011) referred to as makerspace.

Every makerspace is unique and ideally designed to best serve its specific membership. The defining characteristics of all makerspaces are that unique blend of technology with DIY and heritage skills (such as woodworking and textiles). This is what allows for serendipity and innovation.

## Integrating Project-Based Learning, Social-Emotional Learning, and Makerspace

Makerspaces are amazing resources for supporting project-based learning (PBL). A well-stocked makerspace will allow your makers to take their passion projects (a specific type of PBL) to the next level. Adding social-emotional learning gives these an even more powerful dimension, allowing you to focus on the whole child. Merging makerspace, social-emotional learning, and project-based learning helps you to arm your students with the skills to successfully navigate this challenging and ever-changing world.

## Who This Book Is For

This book is aimed at educators working with kids in grades 3–6, developing or already using a classroom or school library makerspace. However, projects included in this book work well for educators, makerspace coordinators, homeschoolers, and even scout troop leaders with kids in grades 3–6, to teach social-emotional skills through makerspace and passion projects. The projects in this book are linked to CASEL's Social-Emotional Learning Framework: Social Awareness, Relationship Skills, Responsible Decision-Making, Self-Management, and Self-Awareness.

## How This Book Should Be Used

This book does not need to be read sequentially. Feel free to skip around to parts that are of particular interest to you, and would work well for *your* makers. The projects contained in this book can be used as is, or adapted for your specific needs.

## What's in the Chapters?

The first four chapters contain projects linked to social-emotional learning skills and include step-by-step instructions, handouts, and additional resources. The fifth chapter takes you from start to finish through scaffolding passion projects. The last two chapters focus on management: funding and supplying your makerspace, grant writing, organizing and managing your makerspace, and making sure your space feels inclusive. Here are more specifics.

### Chapter 1: Use Cardboard to Build Community

Useful tools for cardboard construction. Basic safety information. Establishing student-driven guidelines for safety and respect in makerspace. Detailed project plans for making giant dice and hosting a cardboard building challenge. Thoughts about how to be inclusive with gaming night. Information about how to use these to build community. Prototyping an inclusive playground. Teach kids to be Socially Aware and Self-Aware. Show kids how to become Responsible Decision-Makers.

### Chapter 2: Use Paper to Spread Kindness and Raise Awareness

Make handmade cards out of recycled paper, for good causes. Level them up by adding paper circuits. Teach kids to think about spreading kindness, brightening someone's day, and the reasons why this is so important.

### Chapter 3: Use Fabric to Help Others in Your Community

Make simple scarves and neck warmers for the homeless. Make a tie pillow for a shelter pet. Help kids think about others' experiences. Teach kids about empathy, and having a growth mindset, perseverance, and grit.

### Chapter 4: Share Our Stories and Learn about Others through Audio and Video Production

Teach kids to create videos to share their stories and podcasts to raise their voices. Learn several techniques for how to create a green screen. Help kids create their own, customized, virtual calming room. Teach kids to become Self-Aware and help them to develop Social Awareness by listening to and watching other kids' podcasts and videos.

### Chapter 5: Facilitate Passion Projects

Help kids discover their own passions, and leverage them to help others in their school, community, or even the whole world. Use passion projects to teach kids collaboration and reflection skills. Help them explore their goals and values. Teach them to value each other and work together to pursue a collective goal.

### Chapter 6: Fund and Supply Your Makerspace

Some specific suggestions for a variety of ways to obtain materials that you may not already have but that would be very useful in your makerspace. Includes information about grant writing.

## Chapter 7: Management, Trainings, and Volunteers
Steps to take to keep things running smoothly including the use of lanyards, badging, and training your students to mentor others. Management strategies for safety, and information about how to recruit, guide, and support your volunteers.

## Synopsis

*Social-Emotional Learning Using Makerspaces and Passion Projects* is a practical guide chock-full of ideas that you can put into practice immediately. Included in this book are a repository of resources, including step-by-step instructions, handouts, and reproducibles. The content in this book is based upon thousands of hours of training and experience with makerspaces, passion projects, project-based learning, and social-emotional learning in K-12 settings.

I hope that *Social-Emotional Learning Using Makerspaces and Passion Projects* excites and inspires you, and your makers. Use the ideas contained in this book to teach kids how to be innovative, inclusive, and empathetic. Teach your makers to recycle, raise their voices about causes they care about, make decisions responsibly, and mentor others. Guide them in spreading kindness, and helping their community. Use this book to teach them the social-emotional skills they need to succeed in life.

# Chapter 1

# Use Cardboard to Build Community

Makerspace activities build community. Being part of a community is important for well-being and gives your makers the chance to practice Social-Emotional Learning (SEL) skills related to Self-Management, Social Awareness, Relationship Building, and Responsible Decision-Making.

The projects in this chapter were chosen because they are inclusive, fun, and can be utilized with any age group. When working with makerspace, just like in any classroom, community building is where you should always start. Safety should also be at the forefront. In addition to projects using cardboard, this chapter discusses establishing safety rules, and provides an overview of different cardboard cutting tools, why you would use one over another, and what they are best for.

## Projects, Activities, and Resources Included in This Chapter

- Activity 1: Establishing Safety Rules
- Handout: General Makerspace Safety Rules
- Handout: Stop – Breathe – Look and Think
- Handout: Tips for Using Makedo Tools
- Project 1: Make Giant Dice for a Gaming Night
- Project 2: Host a Cardboard Challenge
- Reproducible: Our Makerspace Is Hosting a Cardboard Challenge!
- Handout: Cardboard Challenge Reflection

## Safety Considerations

### Activity 1: Establishing Safety Rules

Estimated time: 30–60 minutes (time varies depending upon if you choose to develop your own or adopt established rules).

DOI: 10.4324/9781003238072-1

Learning objectives:

- By the end of this lesson, students will understand, and know how to demonstrate, basic safety considerations needed when working with makerspace tools.
- Students will create and/or adopt a list of safety rules to be used when working with makerspace tools.

Social-Emotional Skills:
Responsible Decision-Making (CASEL's SEL Framework):

- Thinking through the steps needed to complete a project.
- Considering and practicing using tools safely.

Self-Management (CASEL's SEL Framework):

- Making good choices when using tools.
- Regulating impulses.

## Step 1: Gather Your Materials
### What You'll Need

- One of each of the tools you'll be using in your makerspace activities, for demonstrative purposes.
- Copies for all students of the *Stop – Breathe – Look and Think* Handout, with a few extra copies to post near work stations.
- Copies for all students of the General Makerspace Safety Rules, computers, tablets, or paper and pencil if you're planning on developing your safety rules together. Safety rules should also be posted near work stations.

Keeping kids safe around sharp and hot tools is a critical part of managing a makerspace. Focusing on Self-Management and Responsible Decision-Making from the start helps kids to self-monitor around these tools. Just as many educators work with students to create classroom rules at the start of the year, it's a great idea to get your makers involved in creating safety rules before introducing your makerspace. This also gives them ownership. When kids feel ownership, they're much more likely to follow the rules. You'll want to add any important safety rules that they don't think of on their own. Use the General Makerspace Safety Rules as a guide.

Alternately, if you're strapped for time, you can simply adopt the General Makerspace Safety Rules, talk your kids through each of these established rules, and point out the ways in which they apply to your tools, in your space.

## Step 2: Consult Manufacturer-Provided Safety Guides

Make sure to consult and follow any manufacturer-provided safety guides, before you or your kids decide on any rules or start operating any tools. You'll want to read through these before establishing your safety rules.

## Step 3 (Optional): Create Safety Rules Together
If you'd prefer to create your own rules, help students brainstorm some general ideas (you'll need to allow extra time for this).

Here are some questions you can ask, to get them going:

- What should we watch out for when using this tool?
- What can you do to keep from getting poked by this sharp end?
- How much space do we need to work with this tool safely?
- What should you do if you see someone making an unsafe choice?
- What should you do if you or a friend gets hurt?

Thinking through these questions helps students develop skills related to Responsible Decision-Making ("The abilities to make caring and constructive choices about personal behavior and social interactions . . . [including safety concerns]" from CASEL's SEL Framework). Determining which rules are the collective best also aids Relationship Skills ("communicating effectively," "practicing teamwork and collaborative problem-solving").

Write down your makers' answers and collectively decide on rules to use to stay safe in makerspace. Add anything important from the manufacturer-provided safety guides, and your own experiences, which may have been missed.

## Step 4: Post Your Safety Rules
Type up (if applicable) and post the safety rules in visible places around where your makers will be working.

## Step 5: Make a Plan for Unsafe Choices
Make sure you have a plan for what you will do if your kids make unsafe choices. This can be a teacher decision, or something you come up with as a class. Obviously, consequences will depend upon the severity of the unsafe choice. Will they simply need to be redirected? Will they lose the use of that tool for the day? Will they need to work on a non-makerspace activity?

If it's more than one maker using a tool in an unsafe way, you may need to always supervise the use of that tool, or revisit with the whole group how to use it safely. Perhaps it lives on your desk, and makers can only use it when you're watching them. It may also become a teacher-use-only tool where you help them with that particular tool, when they need it for their project.

## Handout: General Makerspace Safety Rules

Always follow instructions carefully. If you don't understand something – ask!

Wait to touch tools/equipment until instructed to do so.

Only use tools that you have been trained to use safely.

Report any accident or injury to the instructor immediately, even a papercut.

Know where the Band-Aids and the first aid kits are.

Always wear protective gear when needed. For example, wear safety goggles when using a hammer or a saw.

Always clean up any messes you make.

Make sure all equipment is unplugged, and put away, before leaving.

If you use anything hot, leave it in the spot reserved for hot items.

When you are in the makerspace, wear closed-toe shoes.

If you have long hair, make sure to tie it back.

## Step 6: Teach Self-Management and Responsible Decision-Making with Stop – Breathe – Look and Think

Place one each of a good representation of tools that you plan to use in your makerspace, on a table or desk in front of you (where it can be viewed by all of your makers). Ask kids to think about how they usually approach using a tool. Do they often just grab it and start working with it, or do they reflect on the best, and safest, way to use that tool? Ask for a show of hands as to which they usually do. Emphasize that a lot of people – adults too – just grab a tool and start working with it. Follow up by telling them that doing it this way causes more accidents, which is why we're going to learn a better way.

Tell them that in order to remember how to use the tools safely we will start our sessions with the *Stop – Breathe – Look and Think* activity. Ask them to think about one of the tools in front of you for this activity. Walk them through the steps in the *Stop – Breathe – Look and Think* handout. The first part of this handout models Self-Management. The latter part of this handout helps reinforce Responsible Decision-Making by having kids predict a safety issue that could impact themselves or others and asks them to problem-solve beforehand.

Ask a few of the students to share which tool they were thinking about, and walk them through their answers from the *Stop – Breathe – Look and Think* handout. Next, have them pair and share (turn to a partner and share) their thinking. Post copies of this handout in visible places near where your makers will be working.

## Handout: Stop – Breathe – Look and Think

Before you start working with any tool:

1. Stop and take a deep breath.

Close your eyes (as long as that's comfortable, otherwise you can just take a nice deep breath with your eyes open).

2. Take a moment to think through the steps for how to use that tool safely. If you can't remember these steps, ask.
3. Open your eyes and look around your space.
4. Ask yourself these questions:
    - Do you have enough space to safely use this tool? If not, how can you solve that problem?
    - What do you need to be careful about in this space to keep yourself and others safe? For example, is there a cord that could be tripped over? If so, pay attention and make sure to warn anyone who might trip over the cord.

## Step 7 (Optional): Act It Out

If you're working with a group that seems to be having trouble with these SEL skills (specifically Self-Management and Responsible Decision-Making), have them perform some skits. Pair students up, tell them which tool they're assigned, and give them the directive of making a safe, or an unsafe, choice. Emphasize that if they have the unsafe scenario, *they aren't actually going to demonstrate it*; they will instead talk through the unsafe choice that was made.

Call them up, one group at a time, and have them act out the scenario. Don't tell the audience, in advance, if they are acting out the safe or unsafe choice. Pause after each demonstration and ask the audience for a show of hands as to whether that was a safe, or an unsafe, choice. Reveal which one it was. Brainstorm with the group about how to make safer choices. Repeat until all tools have been demonstrated. You'll need to allow extra time for this activity.

# Cardboard Construction Tools: Canary, Makedo, and Skil

Cardboard can be used for a variety of maker activities for kids of all ages. Once you have a nice stash of cardboard, you will need some tools to cut it. Here are some tool options with tips on how to teach younger kids how to use them, and why you might choose one over another. In my fifth and sixth grade makerspace we have all of these tools (something you might also consider).

## Makedo Tools

Makedo tools are my favorite to use with big groups of younger makers. Unlike with X-Acto knives, or even scissors, it's almost impossible to hurt yourself using Makedo tools. I've had hundreds of kids use them during our participation in the Global Cardboard Challenge (more on that later). The worst injury that they've ever gotten was the equivalent of a paper cut.

**Figure 1.1** Makedo Tools
Source: Photo by Terry K. Lawrence

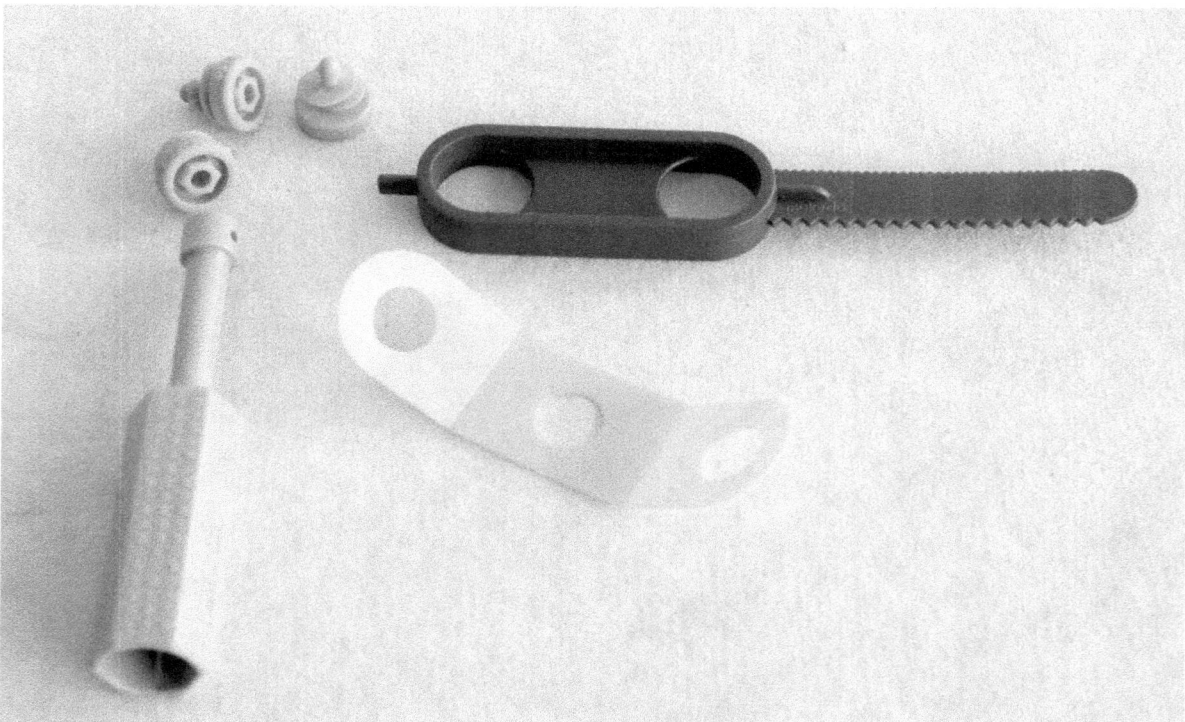

Use Cardboard to Build Community   9

However, the tools *do* need a demonstration in order to understand how to properly use them. They also require some arm strength, especially when working with thicker pieces of cardboard. It helps kids to work with a buddy – one maker to hold the cardboard steady, while the other one cuts it. They can take turns with these jobs.

Figure 1.2 Makedo Safe-Saw

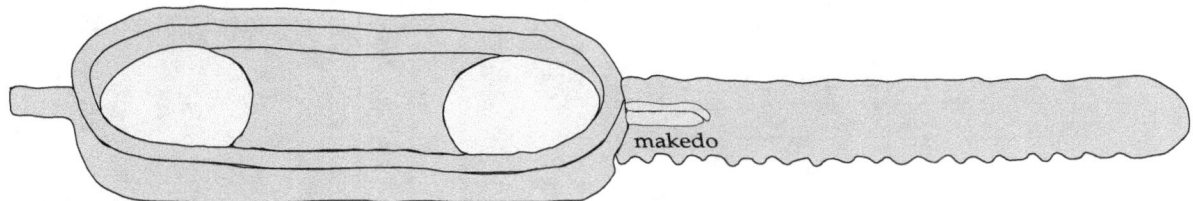

The Makedo Safe-Saw has larger teeth on one side (of the cutting end) and smaller teeth on the other. On the Makedo website they state that the larger teeth are for cutting thicker, corrugated cardboard and the smaller teeth are for cutting thinner pieces like cereal boxes.

However, I've found that the bigger teeth are better for making big cuts, while the smaller are better for more detailed cuts. The opposite end of the Safe-Saw has a tab on the bottom that works well for scoring cardboard before flipping the Safe-Saw over and using the teeth for cutting. This tab is also good for poking holes, which can then be used for the Scrus to screw into. Another use for the tab end is to poke a perforated line for folding the cardboard into a different shape.

Figure 1.3 Makedo Scru-driver and Scrus

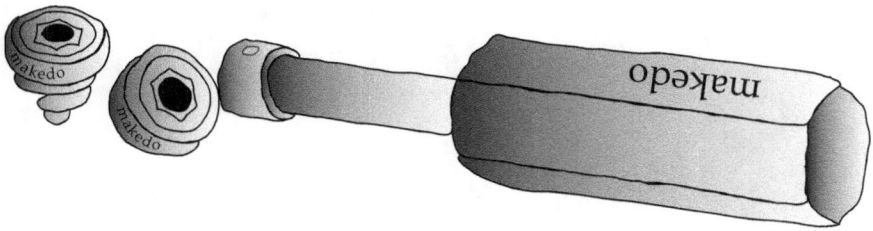

The Makedo Scru-driver works with Makedo Scrus to secure pieces of cardboard together. The thinner end of the Makedo Scru-driver is used to guide the plastic Makedo Scrus into place. The other end of the Scru-driver is a tool that works well for unscrewing and removing the Scrus. Makedo Scrus are used to hold pieces of cardboard together. Although the sets I own are the older model (still available through Amazon for $15 for one starter kit), the newer versions essentially work the same way. Newer versions include the tab to poke holes, on both the Safe-Saw and the Scru-driver tools (older versions, as pictured, only have this tab on the Safe-Saw tool).

10　Use Cardboard to Build Community

## Handout: Tips for Using Makedo Tools

Score the cardboard using the tab end of the Safe-Saw before cutting it with the teeth of the Safe-Saw.

Figure 1.4 Makedo Safe-Saw (arrow identifying the teeth)

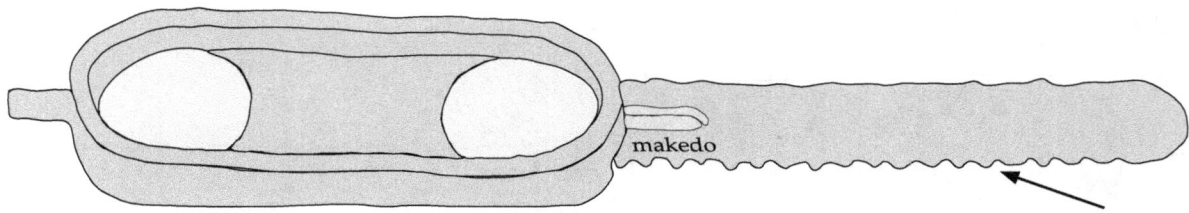

　　Use your body weight to help make the cut. It also helps if a friend is holding the cardboard steady.
　　To poke a hole in the cardboard (for the Scrus, *or* just to make a hole) use the tab end of the Safe-Saw and lift the cardboard slightly off the surface that it's resting on. This will make it easier to get the tab through.
　　Use the opposite end of the Scru-driver to remove the Scru (remember the lefty-loosey, righty-tighty rule).

Figure 1.5 Makedo Scru-driver and Scrus (arrow pointing to the Scru-driver end)

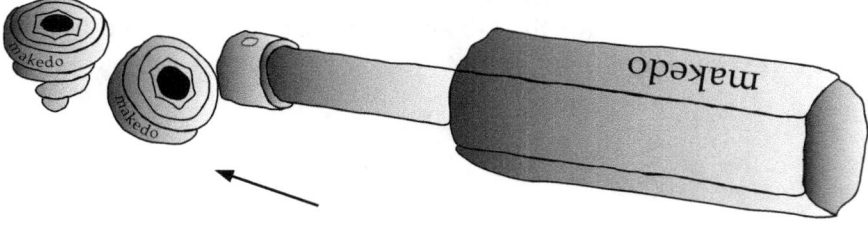

# Canary Tools

**Figure 1.6** Canary Corrugated Cardboard Scissors and Cutter
Source: Photo by Terry K. Lawrence

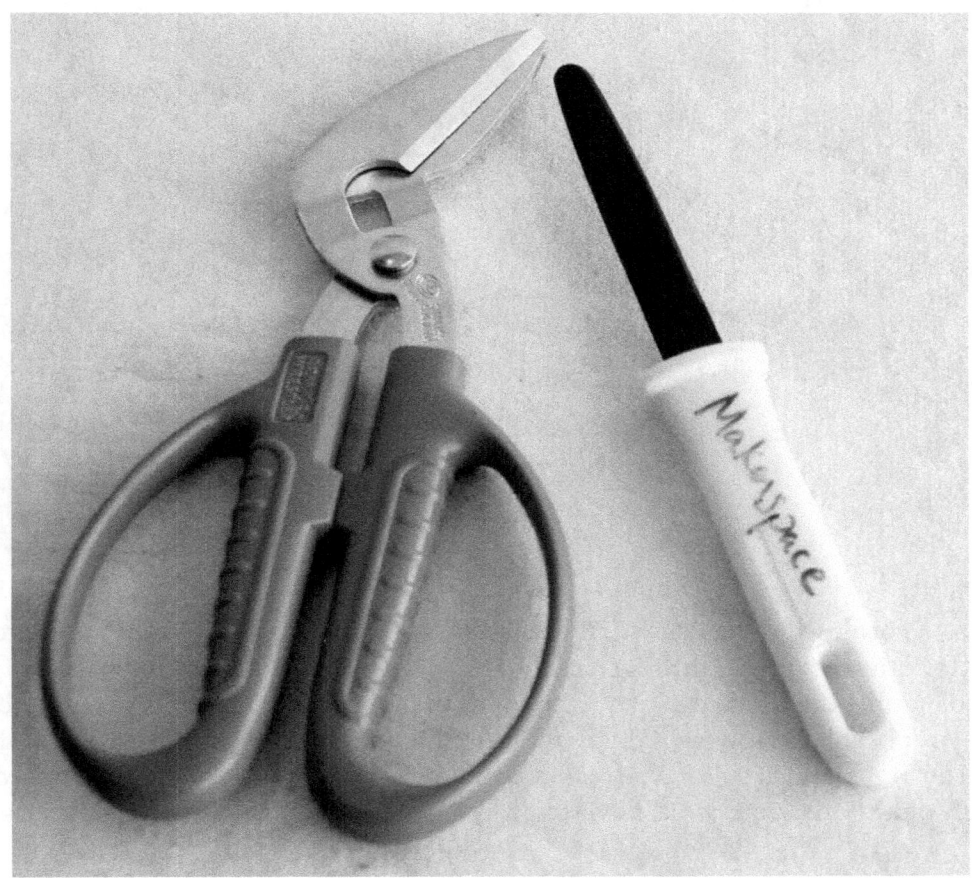

The serrated blades on Canary cutters cut through cardboard quickly and easily. The Canary cutter is harder and stronger than a Makedo saw, so there is more of a chance of a minor injury (you could get a good poke with some momentum), but these are still *much* safer than using utility knives. Canary cutters also require less strength to use than the Makedo Safe-Saw. For thicker pieces of cardboard, I sometimes advise kids to use the scoring end of the Makedo Safe-Saw, and then have them perform the actual cuts with the Canary cutters.

Canary scissors don't hurt your hands as much as other types of scissors do, when you are using them to cut cardboard. The handle is angled, which makes it more ergonomic. As long as kids aren't putting their fingers in the way, they are unlikely to get injured. However, you will want to make sure they aren't forcing the cut. Remind them to take their time since the blades are sharp. Students sometimes want to hold the cardboard on their laps when they are cutting. Remind them this isn't a good idea, and direct them to place the cardboard on the table when cutting.

## Power Screwdriver/Cutter

**Figure 1.7** Skil Cutter
Source: Photo by Terry K. Lawrence

Skil makes a cordless power screwdriver that has a cutter attachment (with a guard) that's excellent for quickly cutting through cardboard. It's fairly lightweight too, making it easier for kids to handle. If you have a lot of cardboard that you want to be able to cut quickly, this could be your best bet. However, if you work with little kids, I'd stick with one of the other choices. The Skil blade is super sharp, and there are easy ways to get past the guard. If you work with older kids, you could have them use this as long as they are supervised while using it.

# Projects Using These Tools

Now that we've covered cardboard tool options and safety, let's move on to some fun projects!

## Project 1: Make Giant Dice for a Gaming Night

Estimated build time: 30 minutes–2 hours.
　Learning objectives:

- By the end of this project students will understand how to create giant dice using cardboard, paper, and tape.
- After making their own dice, students will use these to play games with others.

- Students will develop measurement skills through building giant dice.

Social-Emotional Skills (Adapted from CASEL's SEL Framework):
Relationship Skills:

- Students will work on sharing and taking turns while building their die.

Social Awareness:

- Students will understand that creating large dice can make games more inclusive to others who may have trouble with vision or fine motor skills.

Self-Management:

- Students will have a plan for if they feel frustrated such as taking a break (or using another effective strategy that works for them).

Responsible Decision-Making:

- Students will think through steps needed to successfully complete their die.
- Students will consider why using recycled materials to make new items is a better choice (whenever possible).

Self-Awareness:

- Students will identify if they're feeling frustrated and take breaks or use other strategies that work for them.

The amount of time needed for this project will vary vastly, depending upon: which tools you use to cut pieces out; the age of your makers; whether kids are making one die or two dice; and if you cut the pieces out for them, in advance.

If you're short on time, cut all the pieces in advance using a tool such as the Skil cutter. You could even cut out the papers for the sides using a paper cutter, punch out circles for the dots, and just have them assemble the pieces. Perhaps you could enlist some volunteer help for this. However, if you're using this project to help kids develop measurement and motor skills, you'll want to have them cut everything out themselves.

Making giant dice is an activity that can be enjoyed by any age group. First of all, it's fun. Secondly, giant dice can be used in a variety of ways. They can be used to teach about how to make something cool out of recycled materials (reinforcing Responsible Decision-Making), as an add-on maker activity for a family game night, to use to play kid-created board games, or to reinforce basic mathematical concepts.

Kids can also use these dice to develop activities that are more inclusive for the visually impaired – the bigger the dice, the easier they are to see. Giant dice are easier to handle for anyone who has issues with fine motor skills. They could even be used with your feet (by kicking to roll them) by someone who can't use their hands. Make sure you discuss these advantages to giant dice, to reinforce Social Awareness (understanding others' perspectives/empathy) (CASEL's SEL Framework).

The idea for this project came from a video from the Plano Public Library, Library Make series: http://bit.ly/YTLibraryMake.

## Step 1: Gather Your Materials and Set Up Stations

Note: Double the consumables if makers are building two dice.

### What You'll Need

- Cardboard – enough for each student to make a single 6-sided die. How many boxes will depend upon the recycled box's shape and size. Collect more than you think you'll need; 2–3 boxes per student.
- Ruler – 1 per pair.
- Paper – 6 pieces of plain white and 2 pieces of black construction paper per student. Have extra on hand in case students make mistakes or they make their dots really big.
- Pencil (1 for each student).
- Duct tape (1 roll per work station).
- Scotch tape (1 roll per work station).
- Canary cardboard cutting scissors (1 tool per pair).
- Regular – paper-cutting scissors (1 tool per pair).
- Makedo Safe-Saw (1 per work station).

### Optional

- Paper cutter (adult use only).
- Skil cutter tool (adult use only).
- Large circular paper punch (depending upon how you're creating your dots).
- Markers (at least 1 per student).
- Glue to adhere dots (1 glue stick per pair).

## Step 2: Review Safety and Remind Makers about Considerate Sharing

Safe use of these tools helps students develop SEL skills related to Self-Management and Responsible Decision-Making (CASEL's SEL Framework). Remind them to also consult the posted safety rules (see General Makerspace Safety Rules handout on page 4).

Social Awareness is also needed when sharing tools with others; sharing is one way students learn social norms (a facet of Social Awareness from CASEL's SEL Framework). You may need to circulate and give reminders to students about sharing, to help them to work on these skills. Some students may be impatient to complete their die and reluctant to share tools with their partners.

## Step 3: Break the Boxes Down Flat

Have your makers break the recycled cardboard boxes down, so that they lie flat. You may need to give them a demonstration first. Have them cut or pull off any tape or stickers that they can (easily) remove.

## Step 4: Determine the Size of the Die, and Measure and Cut the First Side

Have your makers decide how big they want their die to be. Have them take turns using the ruler to measure out the first cardboard square. In my example, I made my square 8 × 8 inches. Students should use a pencil to mark the sides, and then cut out the first square. The Canary scissors are a good choice for making these cuts easily, and the tab on the Makedo Safe-Saw tool can be used to score the cardboard before making cuts.

## Step 5: Trace and Cut Out the Remaining Sides

Next, have students trace around that first square, onto additional pieces of cardboard, 11 more times for 2 dice, 5 more for 1. Students should check that their markings are clear. Marks can be made with a pencil or marker. Students should then cut each of these additional squares out.

This is the most time-consuming part of the project, so make sure you allow plenty of time to complete this step. If your makers are in grades 3–4, an adult may need to help, or may even need to cut out pieces for them. If adults are involved in the cutting process, consider having them use the Skil cutter tool, to expedite the process.

Since cutting the pieces is the most time-consuming part of the project, it takes patience. If kids are completing this themselves, before starting this step, give your makers a heads-up that this is challenging. Have them brainstorm strategies for what to do if they start to feel frustrated. This helps them become more Self-Aware and also helps develop strategies for Self-Management.

Pair students up while they're making dice so that whoever finishes first can help their partner. This partnership can help your makers develop Relationship Skills on both sides; one kid asks for (and receives) help and the other provides support, both of which aid in developing positive relationships (Relationship Skills – CASEL's SEL Framework).

## Step 6: Position and Duct-Tape Your Cardboard Pieces Together

Have your makers lay out six cardboard squares in a cross shape and secure the edges with duct tape. Any markings that they don't want to show should face up toward them. Have them duct-tape the edges that touch together. They may need scissors to cut the tape. Remind them to take their time so that tape isn't wasted (Responsible Decision-Making).

**Figure 1.8** Giant Dice
Source: Photo by Terry K. Lawrence

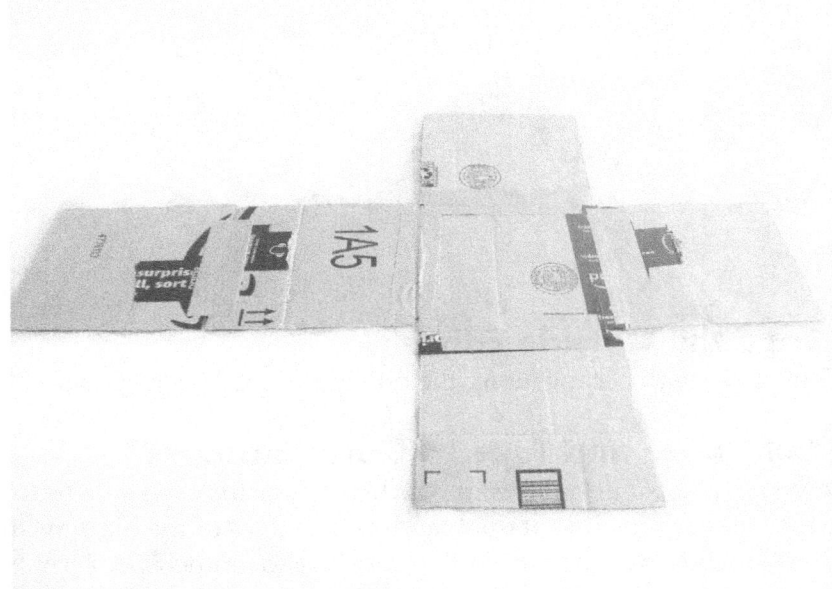

## Step 7: Fold and Tape Your Die Sides into Shape

Once the duct tape is in place, students should fold the pieces inward, taping the edges as they fold them up, to create a cube. Taping the last side is a little tricky. They'll have to secure the duct tape on one side, and then reach inside the die to secure the other side.

**Figure 1.9** Giant Dice
Source: Photo by Terry K. Lawrence

## Step 8: Tape the Outside Edges

Have students adhere duct tape along the outside edges of each cube.

## Step 9: Cut Paper and Tape to Outer Sides

Next, have your makers cut out pieces of white paper for each side (6 for each die). If they want the paper to reach the line of duct tape on the edges of the die, have them cut the paper about a ½ inch smaller than they made the sides. I made mine 7.5 × 7.5 inches (my sides were

8 × 8 inches), and I used a paper cutter to measure and make the cuts. Students can use a ruler, pencil, and scissors to measure, mark, and cut their paper. This is a safer option when you're having kids make the cuts.

## Step 10: Make and Adhere Your Dots

Finally, your makers will need to make the dots. They will need 21 total dots per die. Asking how many total dots will be needed is a good challenge question. Makers can be creative with this part. You may want to encourage your students to use recycled paper (recycling ties into Responsible Decision-Making from CASEL's SEL Framework).

One option for making the dots is to use something circular to trace around (the lid of a small jar would work), and make them traditional, using black paper and cutting them out with scissors. Remind kids that it's okay if they're not perfectly circular; it's difficult to cut a perfectly shaped circle using scissors. I used black construction paper for mine. Students could also use a large hole punch to punch out the dots. They should use glue or tape to secure the dots to the sides. The completed die should look something like this.

**Figure 1.10** Giant Dice
Source: Photo by Terry K. Lawrence

Alternately, kids could make the dots different colors, different shapes (triangles, squares) or even use stickers or pictures of something that they enjoy (pictures of cats, toys, or anything else).

Remind students that a traditional die has sides with dots that number 1 through 6. You'll want to stick to this so that they can be used to play board games.

There are other variations, if you'd like to use what you have on hand. For example, kids can use markers to draw the dots instead of cutting them out of paper. They can make their die entirely out of recycled materials to keep more of the focus on Responsible Decision-Making.

## Celebration

The best way to celebrate this project is to play games with the completed dice. Give students a chance to use their dice to play a game together (this will also help to build Relationship Skills). Playing games with your giant dice is a great option for indoor recess and a means of reinforcing basic mathematical concepts.

Optional: Make your celebration even bigger by hosting a family games night, where families bring in their favorite family-friendly board games, and you swap out the board game dice for your fantastic giant dice!

You could also use these dice with games that students designed and created themselves. Inclusion and relationship building/community building should be the focus of this project, and, of course, having fun.

Using the completed dice to play a game competitively helps teach students about Self-Awareness, because they'll have to think about how they may need to Self-Regulate if they feel big emotions when they lose (or win) games. Also, they should think about how someone else feels when they lose, and not over-celebrate in a way that makes them feel worse. Self-Management (managing their emotions – if they're particularly competitive) and Relationship Skills (specifically communication, positivity, and constructively resolving conflicts) (CASEL's SEL Framework) are both strongly reinforced during this celebration.

# Project 2: Host a Cardboard Challenge

Estimated build time: 3 hours.
Learning objectives:

- Students will work in teams to build something using cardboard.
- Students will work together to determine what they will build.
- Students will define roles and assign tasks needed to accomplish their goals.

Optional:

- Students will assist with organizing an event to showcase their creations.
- Students will research and identify a charity or cause to donate to.

Social-Emotional Skills:

Relationship Skills (CASEL's SEL Framework):

- Students will work on effective communication while building their cardboard project as a team (including listening to and considering everyone's ideas).
- Students will work together to problem-solve and resolve any conflicts that arise.
- Students will ask for help and offer help (respectively) when needed.

Social Awareness (CASEL's SEL Framework):

- Students will recognize each other's strengths, as they relate to different tasks needed to complete their project.

Responsible Decision-Making (CASEL's SEL Framework):

- Students will pay attention to safety and make good choices.
- Students will work together to think through the steps needed to be successful with their project.

Self-Management (CASEL's SEL Framework):

- Students will manage their emotions and try to identify frustrations.
- Students will make a plan for when/if they feel frustrated, and follow that plan.
- Students will set a collective goal of completing their project, and a personal goal of contributing to the completion of the project.

Self-Awareness (CASEL's SEL Framework):

- Students will take a break if they feel frustrated.
- Students will embrace a growth mindset knowing that their first version of their project may not work the way they want it to, that they may need to try different strategies to fix or improve their project.

Cardboard Challenges work really well for kids in grades 3–6. If you want to keep it low-key, simply have kids build something out of cardboard, using their imaginations, individually, in their own time frame.

However, having your makers work in groups adds most of the SEL skills listed above. You can even go big and involve your whole community, and include a donations component (tying in more Social Awareness skills – empathy for those in need). It's up to you.

Cardboard construction is extremely versatile. Kids can create an obstacle course for a toy car or robot, or a marble run to demonstrate forces and interactions. They can build a diorama of a scene from a book or a play. Your makers can try and figure out how to weatherproof a box and create a weather station, or make a cooler to keep items cold.

I've been extremely impressed with what my makers have dreamt up. For example, one pair of students were passionate about constellations. They researched the visible constellations for our hemisphere during that particular season. Next, they mapped out these constellations on the outside of a cardboard box. Using the tab end of the Makedo Safe-Saw, they poked holes to represent each of the stars in each constellation. Next, they drew the constellation figures, in paint, on the outside of the box. Finally, they mounted a flashlight inside the box. We celebrated the finished project by turning out the lights and enjoying our very own DIY planetarium! They used their presentation time to tell some of the stories of the constellations, and describe how to find them in the night sky.

## Step 1 (Optional): Consider Donations

Add another level of SEL by asking community members for an optional donation during the event, which could be given to your school, makerspace, or a local charity. If you choose to do this, work with your makers to decide where the money will go, in advance. Think through who would most benefit from the fundraising. This ties into Social Awareness because it gets kids to think about others' circumstances. Often when requesting donations my students will choose to help a homeless shelter or animal shelter, but a few years back a tornado leveled many of the houses in our community and we used fundraised money (from a book fair) to help those impacted. Add this information to your fliers, emails, social media, and the money collection box, so that community members know who's benefiting from the donations. Empathizing with those in need will motivate your makers and keep the focus of your build on Social Awareness (CASEL's SEL Framework).

Regardless of how you choose to run it, cardboard construction develops design skills and teaches kids to use their imaginations. Working on this project in teams also encourages collective decision-making, compromise, group problem-solving, and a whole host of other SEL skills.

## Step 2: Consider Timing and Storage

If you want to participate in the official Global Cardboard Challenge, you'll need to plan for your build to take place in *early October*. The Global Cardboard Challenge (https://cardboardchallenge.com), also referred to as *Imagination's Day of Play*, is an event that takes place around the world.

Unless you build over the course of one day, and have participants take projects home at the end (which also requires some negotiation as to who gets to take it home, this can help develop Relationship Skills), storing in-process projects will be an issue. You may want to limit the number of pieces of cardboard that your makers are allowed to use, the size of the pieces, or use other parameters that limit build size. Otherwise, you will end up with outsized cardboard forts, or giant obstacle courses that none of the grownups will want to take home with them. Working in groups also limits the total number of projects built, which saves space (and develops SEL skills). You can have your makers break down their projects and put pieces that are still usable back into your makerspace at the end (just make sure you tell them this up front, so it isn't a bad surprise).

## Step 3: Gather Your Materials

You'll need to start collecting materials *at least a month* prior to your Cardboard Challenge.

### What You'll Need

- *A lot* of Cardboard. Consider reaching out to your community for cardboard donations.

- Cardboard construction tools – I would recommend enough Makedo and/or Canary tools that each group has at least 1 set to work with (a set per pair of students is even better).
- Paper and pencil for sketching out design ideas (paper out of the recycling bin works just fine).
- Material to use for sticking the cardboard together; Makedo Scrus, duct tape, and packaging tape all work well for this.
- A plan for materials storage if your build is spanning more than one day.
- Computers, tablets (that they can view on their own), or a computer with a projector (to view as a group) to use to show the short film *Caine's Arcade* (http://cainesarcade.com/).

## Optional

- Crayons
- Markers
- Paint
- Drop cloths
- LED lights
- Coin batteries
- Conductive paint or tape
- Marbles
- Rulers
- Timers
- Physical computing tools such as temperature sensors
- An Ozobot or other type of robot to use in an obstacle course
- Weatherproofing materials such as laminate
- Insulating materials such as foam
- Magnets to use to make your arcade games more complex
- Simple motors to make parts move
- Safety scissors if you're working with littler kids

## Step 4: Make Decisions about Your Event

Your next step is to make some decisions about how you plan to run your event. I find that it works well to have teams of 3–4 students and to give them three work sessions of roughly 45 minutes each. You'll also want to save some time at the end to allow students to enjoy each other's creations. Decide if you're limiting materials, where you'll store the projects in between work sessions, and whether you're going *all-in* with a culminating event open to community members. If you *aren't* hosting a community event, you can skip past steps 5 and 10.

## Step 5 (Optional): Announce Your Cardboard Challenge Event/Fundraiser

The next page is a reproducible that you're welcome to use or adapt. It's a community announcement, which can be made into a flier or shared over social media to help you prepare for your community event.

## Reproducible: Our Makerspace Is Hosting a Cardboard Challenge!

Your student will have the opportunity to participate in our Cardboard Challenge, working with a team to build a structure, out of cardboard, using their imaginations to make it amazing. At the end of the challenge, we would like to invite families to come celebrate and interact with the creations. Although this event is 100% free, optional donations will be collected at the door. Our makers have voted to donate money raised from their Cardboard Challenge to benefit_____

Save the Date!

Family Cardboard Challenge Celebration

Date: _____

Time: _____

Location: _____

We need your help!

In order for our cardboard challenge to be successful, we need materials. Please consider donating the following items: duct tape, packing tape, cardboard boxes (broken down, please).

## Step 6: Set Up Your Challenge

You'll need plenty of space for your makers to work, so choose a big space such as a library or gym, if at all possible. Allow them to work on the floor, should they so choose, so they can really spread out. If you're limiting materials, set up work stations, with tools and materials, in advance. Have rules and safety guidelines posted in clearly visible places, next to stations.

If you're working with younger kids, you may even want to have the cardboard already cut into easily usable pieces, or volunteers on hand to assist. You might also consider only using thin cardboard boxes, such as cereal boxes. Little kids should be able to cut this thin cardboard even just using safety scissors.

## Step 7: Explain, Demonstrate, and Scaffold

Tell your makers up front how many can work together in a group, any materials limitations, and how much time they'll have to build. If you're hosting a community event, they should plan to attend so they can show off their creations. If you're including a fundraiser, make sure to determine where the money will go. You'll want to demonstrate how to effectively and safely use the cardboard construction tools. Review the tips from earlier in this chapter, if you need a refresher. Show your makers the Caine's Arcade video (http://cainesarcade.com/) before they start building. This will help them generate ideas.

Set them up for success by scaffolding SEL skills. Talk about effective communication, remind them that a big part of this project is problem-solving with their group. Encourage them to allocate roles based on each other's strengths. Have them set personal and collective goals. Finally, ask them to think through strategies to use if they start to feel frustrated.

## Step 8: Design and Prototype on Paper

Have students start their projects using pencil and paper, to sketch out design ideas. Have them all create a design, and then either vote on which one should be built, or figure out how to combine their ideas into one design. Point out that even if someone's design isn't chosen for this project, that doesn't keep it from being created. They can always build it themselves, at a different time. Deciding on one design to pursue with a group ties into CASEL's SEL Framework of Social Awareness and Self-Management because you're asking kids to set a collective goal and recognize the value in someone else's design. You may also want to approve the chosen design before letting your makers start building, to confirm that what they're attempting is realistic, given the material and time constraints.

## Step 9: Supervise the Build

Students will need to be redirected if they are making unsafe choices. The building session is where Self-Management will be tested. Your makers should also be celebrated for good teamwork, innovation, and creativity. You'll want to circulate and ask questions. They'll be excited to share their ideas. You may need volunteer help at this point, depending on the age and number of makers.

## Step 10 (Optional): Host a Community Event

If you're hosting a community event you will absolutely need help. You'll need someone to greet and direct community members, someone to supervise the donation box (if you opt for one), and trusted adults to supervise your makers. You'll also want someone circulating and taking photos to share over social media.

You'll need to set a clear start and end time, and make a plan for what happens to the projects at the end of the event. Projects should either be disassembled (and makers should be given enough time to do so), or taken home.

## Step 11: Celebrate and Reflect

Share photos of the groups building, and of their completed projects, over social media to celebrate your innovative makers. Consider taking videos of your makers describing and demonstrating what they've built. You can share these videos using a tool like Seesaw or through an unlisted YouTube channel.

Have students reflect on the event afterwards. I've included a handout for this purpose. One of the questions on the handout asks students to discuss obstacles that were overcome. This question encourages a "growth mindset," an aspect of Self-Awareness in CASEL's SEL Framework.

You might consider making cardboard trophies, and having your community vote on the most interesting, most informative, and most innovative builds. Take a photo with the winning teams, and in addition to posting that on social media, have a physical display, in a visible location, with the photos, and trophies (trophies can be handed off from year to year).

# Handout: Cardboard Challenge Reflection

Name: _____ Date: _____

**Describe what you made:**

**In what ways were you successful?**

**What obstacles did you have to overcome?**

**What did you learn?**

## Conclusion

One of the great aspects of building with cardboard is accessibility. With the proliferation of mail order services (such as Amazon.com), most people have cardboard boxes on hand. Procuring these materials is often as simple as asking your community to save them and bring them in. Free materials not only even the playing field, allowing most to be able to participate, but reusing these materials also helps to teach kids to take a close look at what we discard, and find creative new ways to upcycle materials instead of recycling or even throwing them away.

This helps kids think about making responsible choices (which helps build their SEL skills related to Responsible Decision-Making). In addition, building in teams helps kids develop Self-Awareness, Self-Management, Social Awareness, Responsible Decision-Making, and Relationship Skills (CASEL's SEL Framework). If you take it one step further and collect donations (to give to those in need), another aspect of Social Awareness (empathy) is addressed, too. The options in this chapter are just the beginning.

# Chapter 2

# Use Paper to Spread Kindness and Raise Awareness

In this chapter we'll focus on makerspace projects that use paper and just a few additional tools. We'll make handmade cards out of recycled paper for good causes. We'll discuss how to create paper circuits. We'll use a button maker to create buttons that raise awareness about issues that kids care about. We'll conclude with a prototyping project that emphasizes inclusion. Let's get started!

## Projects, Activities, and Resources Included in This Chapter

- Project 1: Make Handmade Cards from Recycled Paper
- Handout: Guidelines for Writing Cards for Good Causes
- Project 2: Make Your Recycled Card into a Paper Circuit
- Project 3: Make Buttons to Bring Attention to Social Issues
- Handout: Design Your Button
- Project 4: Prototype an Inclusive Playground
- Handout: Design an Inclusive Dream Playground

## Project 1: Make Handmade Cards from Recycled Paper

Estimated time: 1 hour (plus a few days for the paper to dry in between steps).
Learning objectives:

- Students will learn how to make a card out of recycled materials.
- Students will identify ways in which they can use recycled cards to brighten someone's day.

Social-Emotional Skills:
Relationship Skills (CASEL's SEL Framework):

- Students will connect with others through handmade cards.

DOI: 10.4324/9781003238072-2

Social Awareness (CASEL's SEL Framework):

- Students will evaluate why someone might need a "boost" (empathy).

Responsible Decision-Making (CASEL's SEL Framework):

- Students will consider why utilizing recycled materials for this project can help to reduce their carbon footprint.

Self-Management (CASEL's SEL Framework):

- Students will make good choices when using tools and sharing equipment.

Self-Awareness (CASEL's SEL Framework):

- Students will link their feelings and values with the way they express their written thoughts.

In a world dominated by texting and social media, it's a treat to receive a handmade card. Kids can make cards for themselves, to give to friends and family, or as part of a group project (for example, for community outreach or to send to pen pals in another country). Making and sending a card to others to try and brighten their day helps kids develop Social Awareness. If it's someone they're developing a relationship with (friends, family, pen pals), this helps advance their Relationship Skills, too.

## Step 1: Gather Your Materials

### What You'll Need

- Recycled paper (6–8 pieces per card)
- Bowl or jar (1 for each maker)
- A blender
- A window screen cut to size and stapled to a picture frame or a deckle (the official, manual paper-making tool)
- A tub or bin bigger than your deckle or picture frame screen
- A sink
- A sponge
- Towels
- Pencils, pens, markers, crayons, or paint for decorating and writing on the cards after they're made
- Paper and scissors for creating envelopes and cutting the cards to size

### Optional

- Dried flowers, grasses, or other decorative found materials
- An iron
- A hair dryer or heat gun
- Other recycled materials such as magazines, discarded sheet music, or colorful paper

Note: The pulp from the paper takes a few days to dry completely (unless you use a hair dryer or a heat gun to speed things up), so make sure you plan for that. If you do decide to use a hair dryer or heat gun, the edges will curl up more. This can be remedied by ironing your paper (just make sure to place a towel or cloth over it first).

## Step 2: Select Recycled Paper to Re-Use

Have your makers select 6–8 pieces of recycled paper per card. Tell them to keep in mind that selecting paper with a lot of ink will make the recycled cards turn a grayish color. Also, using many different colors of paper can result in what looks like flecks throughout the card. Once they've made one card, they'll have a better idea of the process, and can experiment.

## Step 3: Tear Recycled Paper into Smaller Pieces

Next, give a jar, tray, or other container to each maker, and have them tear the recycled paper into small pieces, roughly 1–2 inches in size. Makers should collect these small pieces in their container.

## Step 4: Blend the Torn Paper with Water

**Figure 2.1** Handmade Cards
Source: Photo by Terry K. Lawrence

30  Use Paper to Spread Kindness

Note: If you only have one blender and one deckle/picture frame, the next few steps will have to be completed one maker at a time. Taking turns, and waiting, will encourage Responsible Decision-Making, Self-Management, and Relationship Skills. Have your makers help make a plan for this.

Have students dump the torn paper into the blender and add enough water to cover the paper. Have them place the blender lid on firmly (you may want to double-check), and pulse until they have a slurry.

## Step 5: Pour Slurry into Deckle/Picture Frame

Have students place the deckle/picture frame screen inside of the tub. Lay a towel out on a flat surface, close by. Makers should pour the paper slurry over the screen. If there are still pieces of paper stuck in the blender, have them put a little more water into the blender, swirl it around, and pour through the screen over the parts that are a little thinner. Repeat until the blender is clean. Have them make sure that the slurry covers the whole screen evenly, and that it comes all the way to each corner. (If it doesn't, they can make more slurry until it covers the screen to the corners.)

**Figure 2.2** Handmade Cards
Source: Photo by Terry K. Lawrence

## Step 6: Add Decorative Elements

At this point, makers can add more decorative elements such as bigger pieces of colored paper, pictures cut out from magazines, newsprint, sheet music, or flower petals. Have them press these pieces down into the slurry to make sure they will adhere. Once everything is placed the way that the maker wants it, have them lift the frame/deckle straight up out of the water and place it on the towel.

Figure 2.3 Handmade Cards
Source: Photo by Terry K. Lawrence

## Step 7: Let Paper Dry

Instruct your makers to leave the paper on the screen for a bit to dry. They can soak up some of the water by gently pressing down onto the paper with a sponge (and squeezing out excess water into the sink). They can speed up the drying process with a hair dryer or heat gun.

## Step 8: Remove Paper from Screen

Once the paper looks like it will stick together (the color is a little lighter than when it was soaking wet, and makers can feel with their finger that it isn't as mushy), students can remove it from the screen. Holding it above a towel, have them flip the screen over and press gently against the back of the screen until the paper falls onto the towel underneath. If the paper falls apart, instruct students to gently press it back together with their fingers.

Students can use a hair dryer or heat gun, again at this point, to try and dry the paper more quickly. Keep in mind that this will make it curl up a little, but you can iron the paper if your maker would like it to be flatter (place a towel or cloth over the top of the paper before ironing).

## Step 9: Cut Card to Size and Personalize

Once the paper is dry, it can be made into a beautiful card! If it's not quite the size or shape kids want (or if some of the slurry didn't adhere), they can cut it to their own specifications, making it a bit smaller, but in the shape that they'd prefer.

If there's enough time, have kids make two cards – one for someone special in their lives such as a friend, teacher, or family member – and one for someone else who might need a pick-me-up. Some great places to send cards include local children's hospitals and organizations that will send them to deployed military personnel; this encourages empathy and the development of Social Awareness. Use the guidelines on the next page to help your makers write out the cards. Feel free to print or adapt this handout.

## Handout: Guidelines for Writing Cards for Good Causes

Here are some ideas for addressing your card (feel free to come up with your own):

- To someone special
- To a brave [kid, soldier . . .]
- Hi there!
- Dear [name]

Make sure that you keep things positive! Some thoughts you might consider:

- You are so brave
- You inspire me
- You rock
- You matter
- You are so valued
- Sending you positive thoughts
- I hope this card brightens your day

You could also think about including an inspirational quote, poem, or story.

Sign the card with your *first name only*. Don't include your last name, email, home address, phone number, or any other personal information.

Don't add any religious sentiments (such as God bless), unless you know for certain that the person you are writing to is religious.

Use the space on the back of this paper to write a first draft of your card. Then copy it over, in your neatest handwriting, onto your handmade card.

## Project 2: Make your Recycled Card into a Paper Circuit

Estimated time: 45 minutes–1 hour.
Learning objectives:

- Students will understand how to create a paper circuit.
- Students will think about creative ways to add their circuit to a card, to make the recipient of the card smile.

Social-Emotional Skills:
Relationship Skills (CASEL's SEL Framework):

- Students will connect with others through handmade cards.

Social Awareness (CASEL's SEL Framework):

- Students will evaluate why someone might need a "boost" (empathy).

Responsible Decision-Making (CASEL's SEL Framework):

- Students will consider why utilizing recycled materials for this project can help to reduce their carbon footprint.
- Students will think through the steps in this project and take their time in order to prevent wasting materials.

Self-Management (CASEL's SEL Framework):

- Students will make good choices when using tools and sharing equipment.
- Students will self-monitor frustration points and make a plan that works for them (for example, taking a break, taking deep breaths, or asking for help)

Self-Awareness (CASEL's SEL Framework):

- Students will link their feelings and values with the way they express their written thoughts.

If you want to take your card to the next level, make it light up with a paper circuit! You can add paper circuits to cards made from handmade paper or regular paper. Since the materials needed to make the card light up (LEDs, coin batteries, copper tape) are slightly more costly, reinforcing Self-Management (not wasting materials) and Responsible Decision-Making (reusing parts from the practice card in the finished card) will be important to this project. Gifting these cards to brighten someone's day (and thinking about why someone might need a little something to lift them up) will help students develop

Social Awareness. This project can be a little tricky, so for some students Self-Management will be key to success, remembering strategies such as taking deep breaths, or taking a break when needed.

## Step 1: Gather Your Materials
### What You'll Need

- Conductive tape. Look for peel-and-stick copper tape in a hardware store or online. Students will need 4 3–4-inch pieces (2 for practice, 2 for their finished card).
- Coin batteries, 3-volt CR2032 work well (1 per student).
- LEDs (1 per student).
- Paper (1 recycled piece for practice, 1 piece – handmade or plain – for final version).
- Scissors (1 per work station).
- Scotch tape (1 per work station).
- Sharp pencils (1 per work station).
- Markers, paint, crayons, or other materials to decorate the cards.

Note: Students should practice creating a paper circuit with recycled paper first. Have your makers start out simply – with just one LED (they can add more LEDs later, as they get more experience). Have them practice first on a plain piece of (recycled) paper. Make sure that they know this first card is for practice only, and they will be taking it apart at the end. Have a brief discussion about how important it is to reuse materials when you can. This emphasizes Responsible Decision-Making and encourages Self-Management (impulse control). Your makers can reuse the coin battery and LED on their final card, once they've had some practice. Slowing them down by having them practice and think through all their steps also reinforces Responsible Decision-Making (CASEL's SEL Framework).

## Step 2: Test the LED
Have kids test the LED to make sure that it's working by pressing the positive lead (the longer one) to the positive side of the coin battery (they should see the plus [+] sign on the battery) and the negative lead (the shorter one) to the negative side of the battery. If the LED lights up, both battery and LED work. If not, you'll need to determine if it's the LED, battery, connection, or some combination of these at fault.

## Step 3: Poke a Hole in the Paper
Next, have students poke a hole through the paper for the LED to push through. They can do this with the end of a sharp pencil. Caution them not to make the hole too big! It should be big enough for the leads of the LED to thread through, but small enough that they can't accidentally pull the top part (the part that lights up) through to the other side. The light will be on the front of their card, and the leads will be on the inside. Since this is practice, if they make the hole too big and the light pulls through, have them try again. Note that they can cover the leads and battery up on the finished version of their card by gluing or taping

a second piece of paper to the inside of the card if they want to make it fancy (after they've completed all of the steps and tested it to make sure it's working).

## Step 4: Bend the LED Leads
Have students bend the leads apart to either side, making a note of which is positive (the longer one) and which is negative (the shorter one). Have them write + and − next to these, in pencil, so that they don't forget which is which.

## Step 4: Prepare the Copper Tape
Students should have two small pieces of copper tape, each 3–4 inches long. If the tape is thick, they can even just cut one 3–4-inch piece, and then cut it in half, lengthwise. Makers should take their first piece of copper tape and remove the paper to reveal the sticky bottom.

This step requires some Self-Management and Self-Awareness. Kids will need to slow down, think through the steps, and double-check themselves. They'll need to make sure they understand where the copper tape goes before sticking it down. Coach them through this by asking them questions: what might go wrong here; what do you need to check first?

When they're ready, makers should stick one end of the copper tape to the practice paper, underneath the negative lead of their LED. They should make sure that the negative lead and one (short) end of the copper tape are touching.

## Step 5: Tape Down the Negative LED Lead
Makers should put Scotch tape over the top of the connected copper tape/LED to make sure they stay connected.

## Step 6: Place the Coin Battery
Next, have kids place their coin battery, negative side down, on the top of the other end of this first piece of copper tape (opposite from the end with the copper tape/negative LED lead). Have students check in with each other, and help anyone who needs it. This develops Relationship Skills.

## Step 7: Connect the Second Piece of Copper Tape to the Positive LED Lead
Students should remove the paper from their second piece of copper tape. They should stick one end of the copper tape underneath the positive lead of their LED, *but don't have them Scotch tape it down this time.*

*Have them also double-check that their two separate pieces of copper tape don't touch.* If they do, that will create a short in their circuit, which means their LED won't light up.

Figure 2.4 Paper Circuit
Source: Photo by Terry K. Lawrence

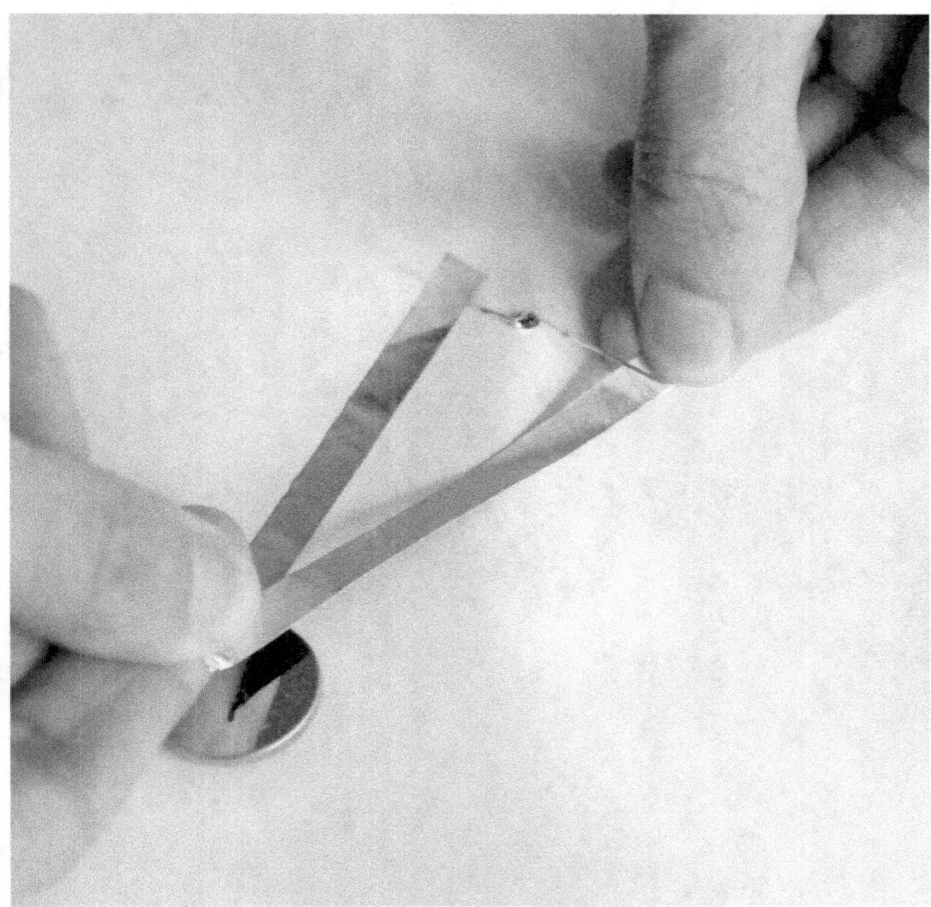

## Step 8: Connect the Other End of the Second Piece of Copper Tape to the Positive Side of the Coin Battery

Have your makers tape the other end of their second piece of copper tape to the top of the coin battery (the positive side). Direct them to secure the copper tape and the coin battery together with a piece of Scotch tape. Once again, have them double-check that the two separate pieces of copper tape aren't touching. This is another great point for a peer check-in.

## Step 9: Bend the Positive LED Lead

Students should bend the positive lead of the LED up slightly, so it's not in constant connection with the copper tape. This will prevent the LED from burning out too quickly and will allow the LED to light up by pressing down from the front of the card. Your makers might include a message on the opposite (front) side of the card that says, "Press Here" in their design.

**Figure 2.5** Paper Circuit
Source: Photo by Terry K. Lawrence

## Step 10: Take Practice Pieces Apart

Now that students have had success with the plain practice paper, it's time to try it on an actual card. Keep at least one successfully completed card as an example for kids to look at as they work. Have them take their practice card apart to reuse the coin battery and LED (reinforcing Responsible Decision-Making).

## Think about Recipients and Repeat Steps Above

Before creating the final version of the light-up card, have students take a moment to think about who they're going to give it to, and why. This will keep the main focus of this project on developing Social Awareness and Relationship Skills.

## Celebration

Share your good work with the world! Take photographs of the completed cards (individually or in a group) and post them on social media. Make sure to also share any acknowledgements by the recipients of the cards with your makers.

## Project 3: Make Buttons to Bring Attention to Social Issues

Estimated time: 30–45 minutes.

Learning objectives:

- Students will communicate a concise message, using words and images, about an issue that they care about.
- Students will combine these into a button (or button style) design.
- Students will use their button to communicate about an issue that they care about with a real-world, authentic audience.

Social-Emotional Skills:

Relationship Skills (CASEL's SEL Framework):

- Students will interact with each other, while wearing their buttons, and share their messages (utilizing good listening skills and showing respect, even if they don't agree).

Social Awareness (CASEL's SEL Framework):

- Students will make a plan for respectful interactions with others who may disagree with their button/message.

Responsible Decision-Making (CASEL's SEL Framework):

- Students will learn and follow the steps used to create a physical button (and to avoid waste).

Self-Management (CASEL's SEL Framework):

- Students will think about the ways in which they interact with others, whom they may not agree with, and still be respectful.

Self-Awareness (CASEL's SEL Framework):

- Students will identify an issue that they care about.

Button making is a great way for kids to educate others, face to face, about issues that are important to them. If you'd like to keep this low-key, you can create stickers instead of buttons. If you'd prefer a digital route, use a platform such as Adobe Spark Post to create and share digital buttons. However, since tools are at the heart of makerspace (and physical buttons are pretty cool), these project instructions cover using a button maker.

## Step 1: Gather Your Materials
### What You'll Need

- Paper
- A button maker – I use a Neil 2 ¼-inch button machine
- Button parts – make sure that you purchase the correct parts for your machine
- A circular hole punch (the same size as the buttons made by your button-making machine)
- Pens, pencils, crayons, and markers for designing the buttons

## Step 2: Brainstorm
Start by asking kids to brainstorm about causes that matter to them. This works particularly well if they're already primed with discussions about big issues such as climate change, pollution in the ocean, unequal access to resources such as food and shelter, or any local issue that they, or someone they know, are directly impacted by. You could also simply ask your makers – what's your wish for the world?

## Step 3: Create the Design
Once your makers have settled on a topic, have them start working on their design. You're welcome to use the handout on the next page. The template at the bottom will work with a 2.25 punch in a 2 ¼-inch button machine. They can also design on a computer and size it to something that will work with your button machine.

## Handout: Design Your Button

Make a button to help spread the word about a cause that you care about!

### Start by Brainstorming: What Do You Want People to Know?

Maybe your button is designed to educate others about an endangered animal. It could explain something happening in your school or community that needs fixing. Perhaps your button simply illustrates your wish for the world. Write down some ideas for your button's message on the back of this paper.

### Pull Out Keywords or a Startling Statistic

From the notes you just made, pull out some keywords or write a short sentence. Another option would be to include a particularly startling statistic. You don't have a lot of space on your button, so make sure your message is short, and clear.

Now it's time for the design! Draw your design inside the circle(s) below. Use both words and illustrations to share your message.

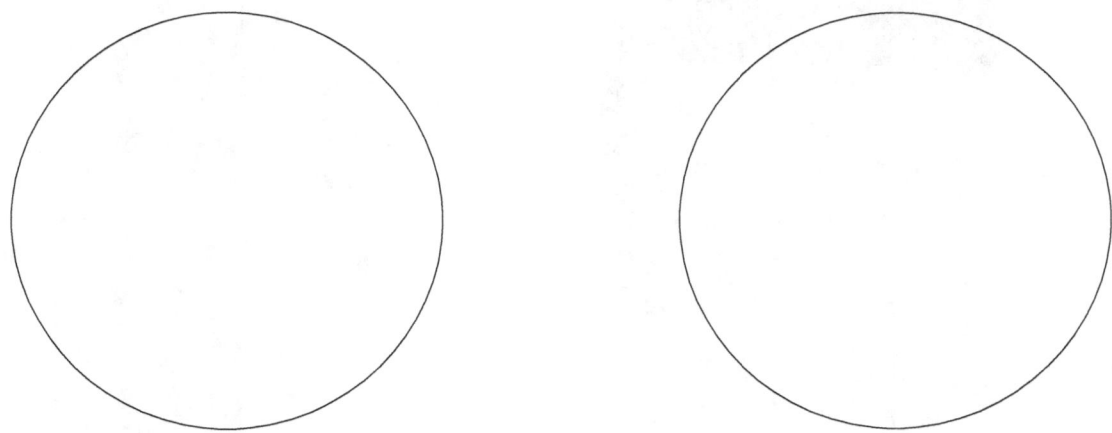

Once the design is complete, it's time to create the actual button.

42   Use Paper to Spread Kindness

## Step 4: Punch out the Paper/Design

Have kids use the circle punch to punch out the design. Have them turn the punch upside-down, so they can see exactly where the edges of the paper will be cut.

**Figure 2.6** Button Making
Source: Photo by Terry K. Lawrence

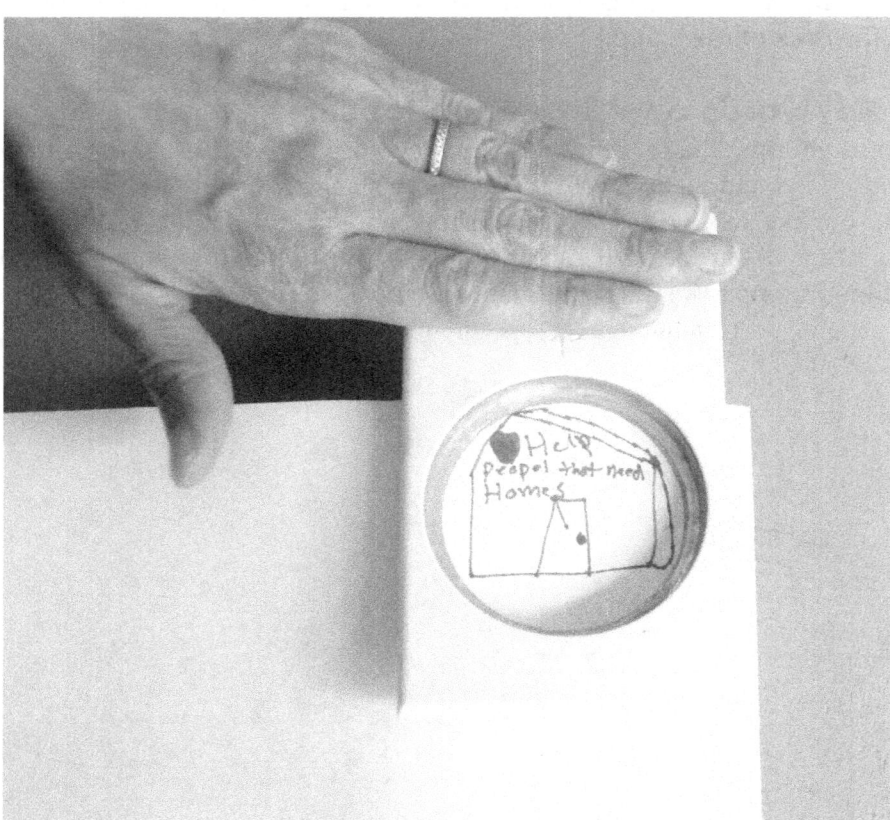

## Step 5: Put the Front Pieces of Your Button Together in the Left Side of the Button Maker Tray

Have kids place (in this order – bottom to top) into the left side of the button maker tray (as they're facing toward it):

1. Shell, face curve side down (have them make sure it's just one, and not more than one, stuck together)
2. The punched-out paper design, design side visible, top of the design facing up
3. A Mylar cover (have them make sure it's just one, and not more than one stuck together)

Slide the tray to the right, until it's underneath the press.

Figure 2.7 Button Making
Source: Photo by Terry K. Lawrence

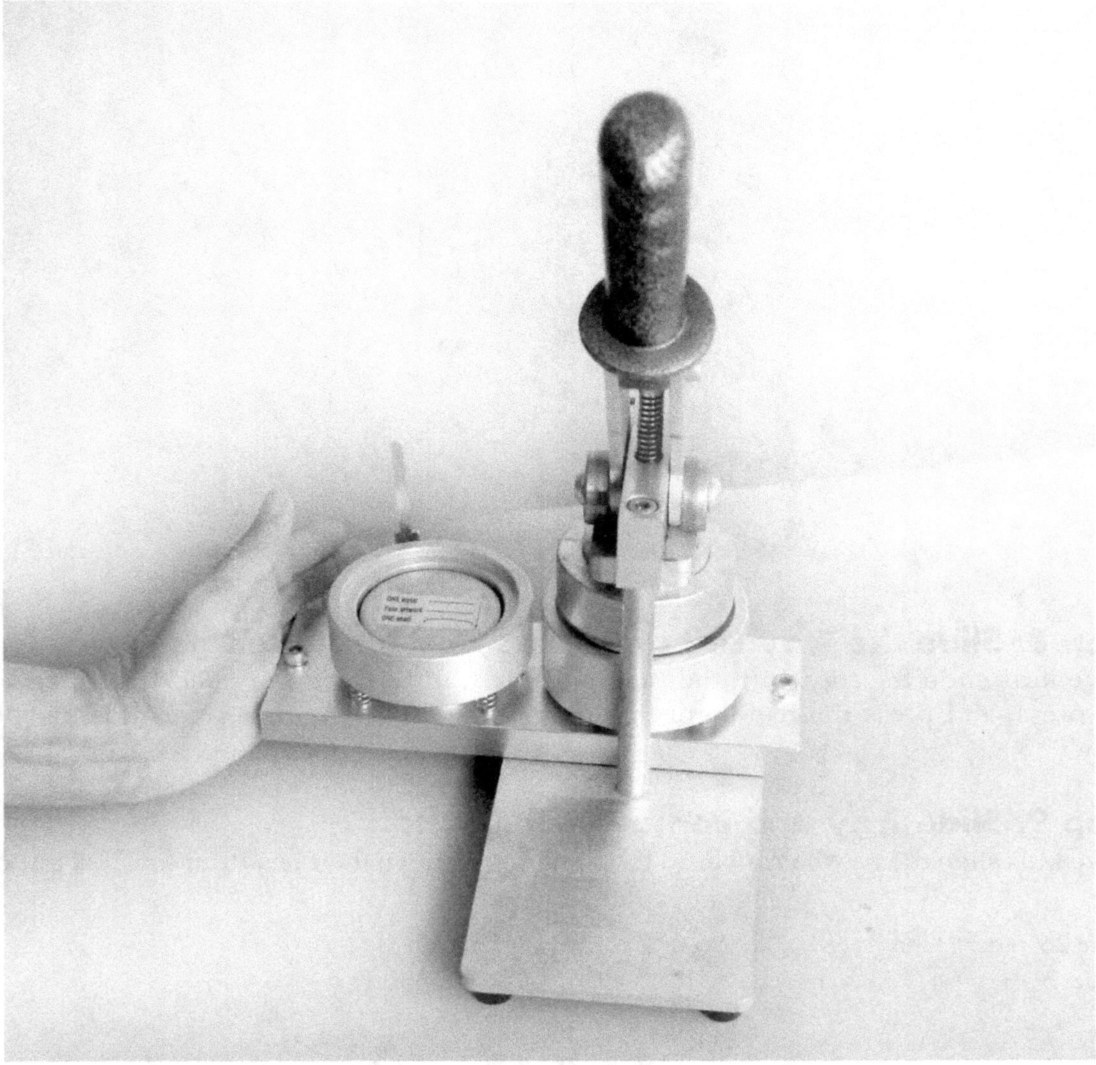

## Step 6: Press down the Button Maker Handle – Firmly

Have your makers press the handle, firmly, all the way down (the shell, design and Mylar should stay up inside the top part of the press). I often tell kids to press down the handle for a count of 3, which helps them to hold it down firmly enough to be successful.

## Step 7: Put a Button Back into the Right Side of the Machine

Have kids place a button back in the right side of the button machine tray, with the pin side down, "squiggly" side up.

**Figure 2.8** Button Making
Source: Photo by Terry K. Lawrence

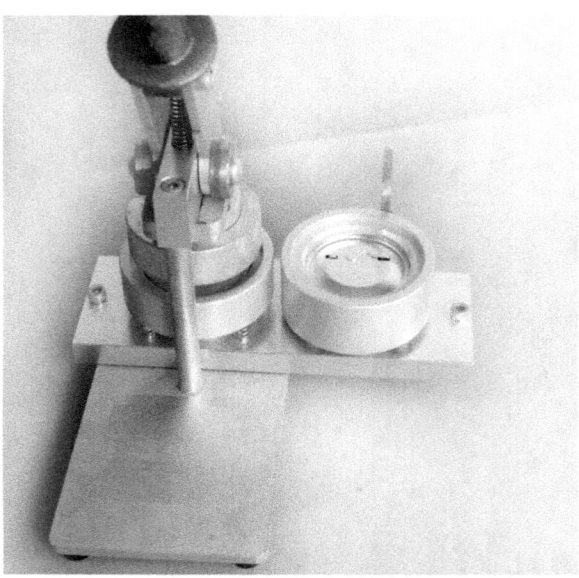

## Step 8: Slide the Tray Left and Press Down the Handle
Have kids slide the tray with the pin, to the left, until the button back is underneath the press, and press the handle of the lever *firmly* down. Again, have students count slowly to 3.

## Step 9: Slide Tray and Remove Your Button
Have kids slide the tray back over to the right and remove their beautiful finished button!

**Figure 2.9** Button Making
Source: Photo by Terry K. Lawrence

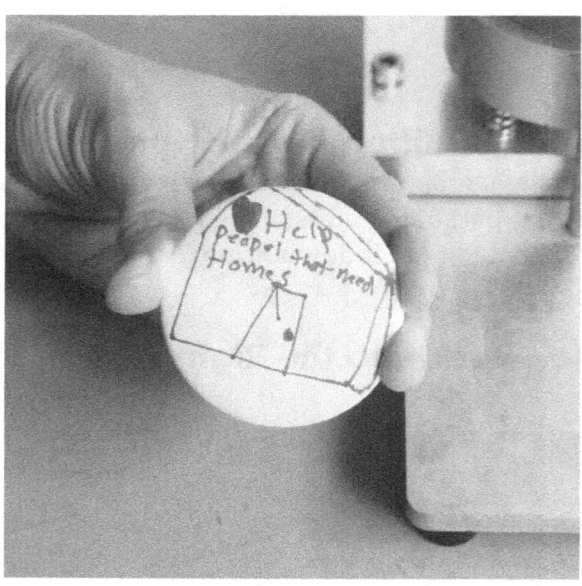

## Celebration

Start your celebration by having your makers wear their buttons and share their messages with each other.

Before you start, set some ground rules that focus on SEL skills:

- Each maker gets 1 minute to share why they made their button, or anything else about their button that they feel comfortable sharing.
- The other person will use good listening skills (turn-taking/Self-Management):
  - They won't interrupt.
  - They'll listen with an open heart.
  - They'll ask at least one thoughtful follow-up question.

(These teach Self-Management, Social Awareness, and Relationship Skills.)

- The listener and speaker will switch roles, and this process will repeat.
- When both partners have shared, they'll each pair up with someone else.

Be sure to allow enough time for everyone to share with several other makers.

Another great celebration for button making is to have your makers wear them out in the world. Consider tweeting out snippets of any thoughtful conversations influenced by the buttons.

You can also create a Word Cloud to share over social media by having students type their button's message into a *Poll Everywhere* (https://www.polleverywhere.com/) that you've set up in advance (or another similar tool).

# Project 4: Prototype an Inclusive Playground

Estimated build time: 1 hour.

Learning objectives:

- Students will understand and apply the concept of Universal Design.
- Students will use these considerations to prototype an inclusive playground.

Social-Emotional Skills:

Relationship Skills (CASEL's SEL Framework):

- Students will collectively decide on a final design with Universal Design in mind.

Social Awareness (CASEL's SEL Framework):

- Students will empathize with kids who can't use traditional playground equipment (and brainstorm solutions).
- Students will consider inclusivity with playground design.
- Students will identify playground equipment that anyone can use, including kids who have a disability.

Responsible Decision-Making (CASEL's SEL Framework):

- Students will think through how different types of playground equipment will or will not work for different people.

Self-Management (CASEL's SEL Framework):

- Students will make good choices when using design tools.

Self-Awareness (CASEL's SEL Framework):

- Students will work to identify their feelings if their design isn't chosen (with a goal to think about what's best for all).
- Students will work on having a growth mindset when working through playground prototype iterations.

Prototyping is an important part of design thinking, which is integral to makerspace. It's important to introduce prototyping as a safe, quick, and inexpensive way to work through initial ideas. Prototyping makes taking risks less scary, which can lead to true innovation. Working through iterations and acknowledging that mistakes are okay and improvements can be made also encourage a growth mindset. Having a growth mindset is part of Self-Awareness (CASEL's SEL Framework).

Prototypes are also great for showing other people the ideas in your head. When I talk to kids about why they should prototype, I often ask them if they would hire a builder to build their house, if that builder *just told them about* what she was going to build, instead of showing them blueprints or a 3D rendering. Obviously, the answer is no. This leads to a discussion about why prototyping saves you time, money and frustration.

Prototyping will look different depending on the age of the makers. In early elementary it may simply mean you ask kids to "draw it first." Older makers may be using K'nex, 3D printers, laser cutters, or other sophisticated tools.

Sometimes prototyping on paper is as far as we get. This is completely fine. When I coach kids through passion projects, their final project could also be to build a 3D prototype. This is also great. When a prototype is the furthest we can take the design due to lack of materials, equipment, or time, I tell them to think of their audience as potential investors in their company. The objective is to convince the "investors" to spend money on *this* invention. This is a great way to merge prototyping and design thinking with creating a persuasive presentation. Not only does it provide a real-world connection, but it also hits lots of standards along the way.

## Step 1: Gather Your Materials

For this project, the simplest way to prototype is to start with pencil and paper. Once you've got a great idea on paper, consider branching out to a 3D version using Popsicle sticks and hot glue, cardboard, a 3D print, or some combination of these.

## What You'll Need

- Paper – several pieces for each student
- Pencils – 1 per student

## Optional

- 3D printer
- Computer to use for 3D design – 1 per student or 1 per pair
- An account to use 3D design software; TinkerCad is a good choice (and it's free) – 1 per student
- Popsicle sticks – 1 box per work station
- Hot glue and hot glue guns – 1 glue gun and 3–4 glue sticks per work station
- Cardboard and cardboard cutting tools – a set per student or pair of students
- Markers, paint, pens, crayons, colored pencils – a selection at each work station

## Step 2: Establish a Real-World Connection

A great way to engage kids is to give them a project with a real-world connection. Smaller kids love playing on playgrounds, and older kids will often have fond memories of this. Asking your makers to create a prototype of a playground design will pique their interest. In a perfect world, you might be able to combine this with a real-life design or redesign of a playground, which the makers will have access to through their school or community. You could take the top designs created by students and submit them to builders as inspiration.

## Step 3: Emphasize Inclusion

For this project you are also going to have kids think about inclusion. When your makers are inventing their dream playgrounds, they should think about how they can make certain that their friends who have a disability can enjoy the equipment, too. This will reinforce SEL skills that fall under Relationship Skills and Responsible Decision-Making (CASEL's SEL Framework). Use this project to introduce Universal Design – and explain that this is something that builders use in the real world – they design buildings that are accessible to everyone. Kids in wheelchairs is a good example of when Universal Design is used. You would want to tell your students to think about how they can make every piece of playground equipment wheelchair accessible. Have them also consider who else could benefit – maybe someone whose leg is in a cast from a broken leg? This is how Universal Design works; when you design with everyone in mind, sometimes others benefit unexpectedly. Have your makers brainstorm other situations that can make it hard for some kids to use equipment. Use the handout on the following page to scaffold this project. As an extension activity, consider bringing your kids out to a piece of playground equipment and using bandannas across their eyes to obscure their vision. Bring extra adults with you to monitor the kids to make sure they are safe. After 10–15 minutes, have them remove the blindfolds, and reflect. Have your makers pair up to share what was challenging. Then bring everyone together for a full group discussion about the challenges of trying to use the equipment with the blindfolds. This is a great way to reinforce Social Awareness (CASEL's SEL Framework) and also have kids think about specific ways to develop a piece of equipment using Universal Design. (This helps kids develop Responsible Decision-Making skills – CASEL's SEL Framework.)

## Handout: Design an Inclusive Dream Playground

Today, you are going to prototype a dream playground. Think about what kinds of structures you like to play on, and how you could make them even better. Write or draw some ideas below.

Next, think about how to make sure your playground is safe and accessible for all of our friends.
Consider:

What kind of structures can the playground include that your friends who are wheelchair-bound could also use?
What about a friend who is missing an arm or a leg?
How can you make sure that the playground is safe for your friends who are deaf or blind?
In the space below, write some of the things that you will need to consider. Once you come up with some thoughts, turn to someone next to you and share ideas.

On the back of this paper, sketch out a dream playground that everyone will be able to enjoy. Start by thinking about a piece of playground equipment that you enjoy. How can you change or add to it so that anyone can enjoy it?

## Celebration

Display your makers' playground designs in a visible area. Post photographs of the designs on social media, with details about how they were designed to be inclusive. Consider including information about how students learned about Universal Design, and if you tried the extension activities, you might include some quotes when exploring the challenges of using a piece of equipment that wasn't developed using Universal Design.

# Conclusion

You don't actually need impressive and expensive equipment to run an effective makerspace. In fact, starting with paper, a few additional tools, and a bit of creativity can lead to thoughtful, meaningful projects. Use the projects in this chapter to help kids think about others, develop a better understanding of Universal Design, spread kindness, and cover a whole host of standards along the way. In the next chapter we'll look at ways to use fabric to help others in our community.

# Use Fabric to Help Others in Your Community

**Chapter 3**

In this chapter we'll explore projects that use fabric to help others. We'll show how to make a simple, classic scarf and a neck warmer that you can gift or donate. We'll also cover how to make a tie pillow to use as a pet bed. These can be gifted to someone you care about, or given to help others in your community (or maybe both). The classic scarf and the tie pillow are both no-sew projects. No-sew textile projects require minimal tools, and any makers old enough to use sharp scissors will be able to complete them.

Textiles are a critical part of makerspace. Having a textiles section both broadens available options, and is welcoming to your makers who may be intimidated by robotics or machines. Textiles make your makerspace feel more inclusive. Most of us have some familiarity with textiles from making friendship bracelets, or sewing on a button. The textiles section of any makerspace is both a destination for learning more sophisticated applications, and a gateway to other types of making.

For simplicity, I've just included projects using fleece. Fleece is forgiving of messy stitching or cuts, and it's warm and soft, which makes it a great choice for kids. A special thank-you to fashion designer Nettie Tiso (http://www.jeannettiks.com/) for her classic scarf and neck warmer patterns.

## Projects Included in This Chapter

- ♦ Project 1: Simple Classic No-Sew Scarf
- ♦ Project 2: Infinity Scarf/Neck Warmer
- ♦ Project 3: No-Sew Tie-Pillow Bed for a Shelter Animal

## Project 1: Simple Classic No-Sew Scarf

Estimated build time: Approximately 30 minutes.
Learning objectives:

- ♦ Students will create a simple, classic scarf, using fleece.
- ♦ Students will practice measuring skills while making their scarf.

Social-Emotional Skills:
Relationship Skills (CASEL's SEL Framework):

DOI: 10.4324/9781003238072-3

♦ Students will work with others to share tools.

Social Awareness (CASEL's SEL Framework):

♦ Students will consider gifting or donating their completed scarf to someone in need.

Responsible Decision-Making (CASEL's SEL Framework):

♦ Students will think through the steps needed to complete the scarf and take their time, so they don't waste fleece.

Self-Management (CASEL's SEL Framework):

♦ Students will make good choices when using tools (such as sharp scissors).

This project is quick, only requires a few tools, and you will end up with a lovely, warm scarf to keep, gift, or donate. Do this project with makers who are old enough to use sharp scissors independently.

## Step 1: Gather Your Materials
### What You'll Need

♦ Sharp scissors (used only with fabric) – 1 per student is ideal, but 1 per pair will work.
♦ 1 yard of fleece (½ yard will work in a pinch) per maker. Unless the pattern is the same for all of your fleece supply, have a few extra yards available so that students have a choice.
♦ Yard stick or quilter's ruler (1 per work station)
♦ Pencil, chalk, or water erasable fabric pen (1 per work station)

Note: You may want to double the consumables for this project and extend the allotted time to 45 minutes–1 hour. That way students can make two scarves – one to keep and one to gift or donate.

## Step 2: Distribute Fleece

Makers need to find a piece of fleece that is long and wide enough to work as a scarf for the recipient. A standard size would be 36 inches long and 6 inches wide.

If you're providing fleece in different colors or patterns, give kids some time to pick out which they'd like. Have a plan for kids picking the same pattern, if there isn't enough material for everyone who wants it. I often just choose a number between 1 and 10, and have the kids guess my number. Whoever guesses closest to my number gets to choose first.

Have your makers lay their material out onto a flat surface, and look at the pattern that they've chosen. The width of the scarf will be determined by how wide your makers like their scarves, and by the pattern of your fabric. For example, if your fleece has an animal in

52  Use Fabric to Help Others in Your Community

the pattern, you may not want to cut it in such a way that you are cutting the animal in half. If makers are cutting scarves from the same piece of material, they should pair up to share cutting and measuring tools. Thinking these steps through before starting this project also reinforces Responsible Decision-Making (CASEL's SEL Framework).

## Step 3: Measure Out the Material
Have kids measure out the length and width of their fleece scarf with a yard stick or a quilter's ruler. They should mark along the edges that they need to cut, to get it to the size they want it. They can use a pencil, chalk, or a water erasable fabric pen to mark their measurements. Just have them use whatever's on hand.

## Step 4: Cut Out the Basic Shape
Have your makers cut along their length and width markings with scissors (used only with fabric).

**Figure 3.1** Classic Scarf
Source: Scarf design by Nettie Tiso

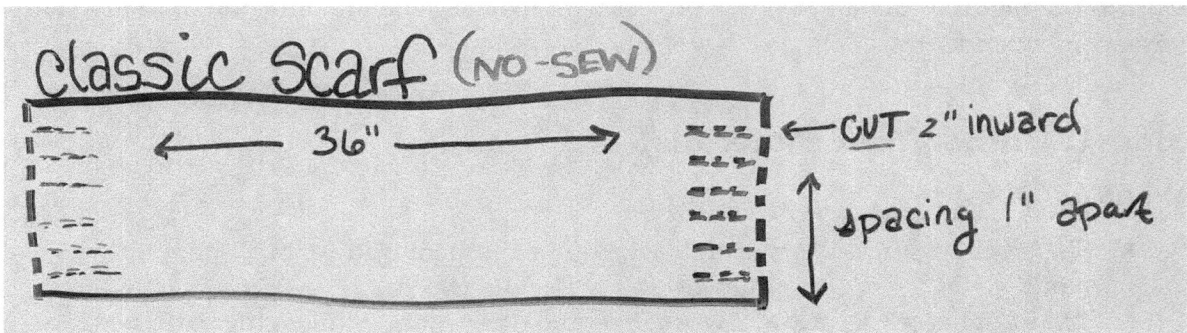

**Figure 3.2** Classic Scarf

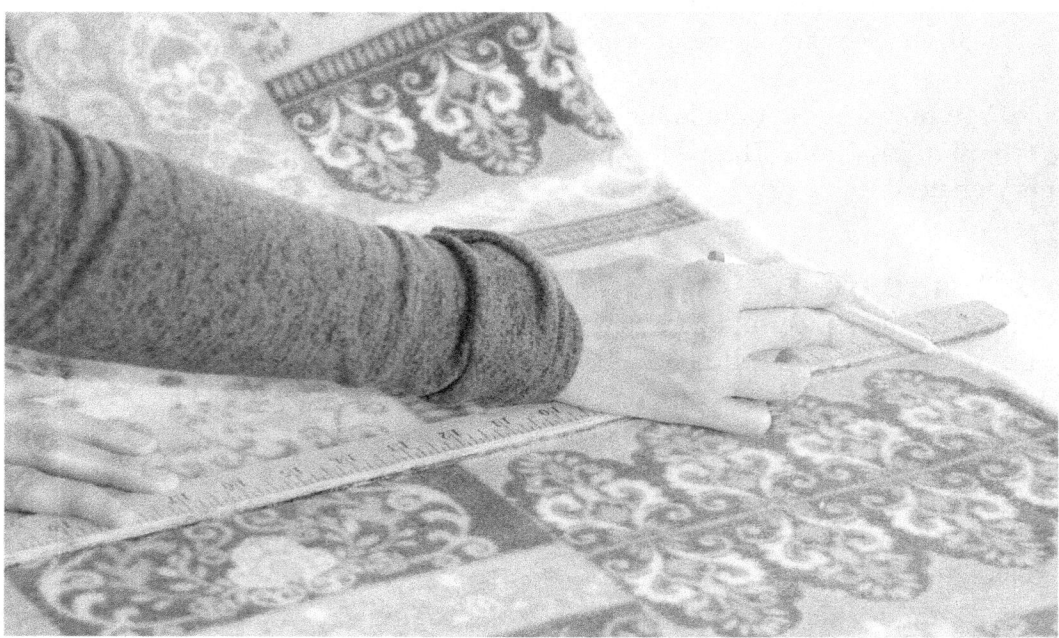

### Step 5: Cut the Fringe

Now that they've got the basic shape of their scarf, it's time to create the fringe. Have them mark a line 2 inches in, on both short ends of the scarf (or longer, if you'd like a longer fringe). Next, have them make dots, 1 inch apart, along the line. They should cut a fringe on both ends by making 2-inch cuts, 1 inch apart, cutting from the edge, to the dots they marked along the line.

Figure 3.3 Classic Scarf

### Step 6: Wash Your Scarf

Kids should wash their scarves before wearing or gifting, to get the measuring markings off.

### Celebration

Make sure you take photos of someone modeling your makers' lovely scarves to post onto social media. Be sure to include positive quotes about the scarves from the recipients, too. Share information about donations – how many scarves were donated and where they were donated.

## Project 2: Infinity Scarf/Neck Warmer

Estimated build time: 45 minutes–1 hour.
Learning objectives:

- Students will use measurement tools to measure material for an infinity scarf.
- Students will use basic sewing skills to sew the ends of the scarf together.

Social-Emotional Skills:
  Relationship Skills (CASEL's SEL Framework):

  ♦ Students will work with others to share tools.

  Social Awareness (CASEL's SEL Framework):

  ♦ Students will consider gifting or donating their completed scarf to someone in need.

  Responsible Decision-Making (CASEL's SEL Framework):

  ♦ Students will think through the steps needed to complete the scarf and take their time, so they don't waste fleece.

  Self-Management (CASEL's SEL Framework):

  ♦ Students will make good choices when using tools (such as sharp scissors and sewing tools).

Infinity scarves, also known as "neck warmers," are wonderful to have when it's bitterly cold outside. They are great for keeping your neck warm, and can also be pulled up to keep the entire lower side of your face cozy. These are particularly nice for donating to homeless shelters in locations that have bitterly cold winters (such as here in Michigan).

## Step 1: Gather Your Materials
### What You'll Need

- Sharp scissors (used only with fabric) – 1 per student is ideal, but 1 per pair will work.
- 1 yard of fleece per scarf (½ yard will work if you are making it for a child)
- Yard stick or quilter's ruler (1 per work station)
- Pencil, chalk, or water erasable fabric pen (1 per work station)
- Sewing pins (1 container at each work station)
- Needle and thread (1 per student or pair) or a sewing machine (1 per work station)

## Step 2: Measure Your Materials

If students are making a scarf for themselves, have them measure out a piece of fleece that will fit around their head when the ends are connected. If they're making a scarf to donate to someone else, have them measure 42 inches long (and 18 inches wide) for an adult and 30 inches long (and 15 inches wide) for a kid. Since I was making mine for two kids, I made two scarves from one piece of fleece.

## Step 3: Mark Your Measurements

Have kids mark the length and width that they want their neck warmer to be with a pencil, chalk, or water erasable fabric pen.

Use Fabric to Help Others in Your Community    55

**Figure 3.4** Infinity Scarf
Source: Scarf design by Nettie Tiso

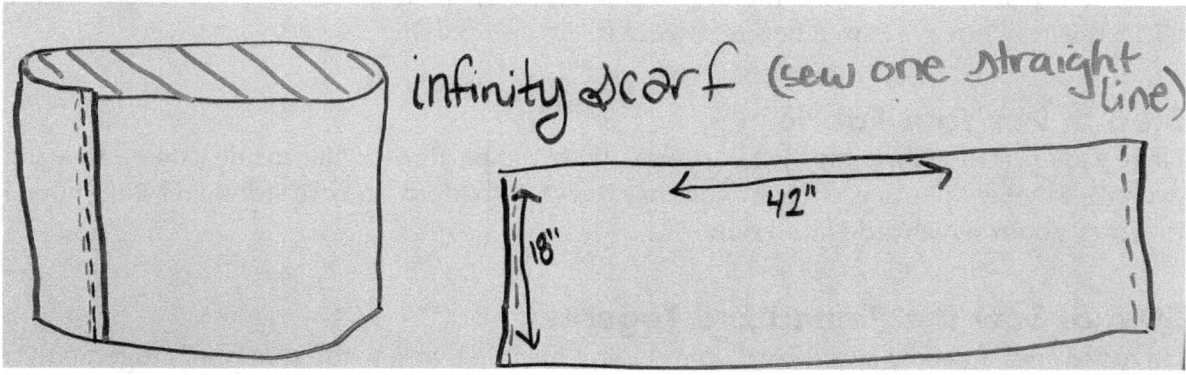

**Figure 3.5** Infinity Scarf

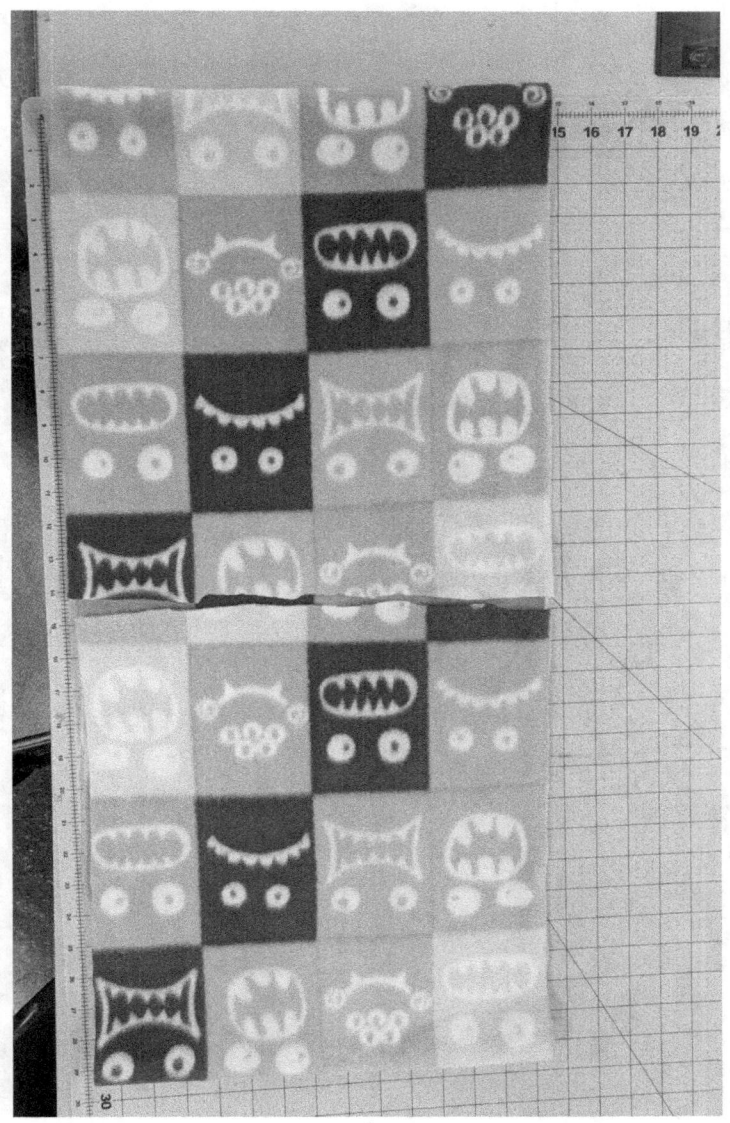

## Step 4: Cut Your Fleece

Have kids cut the fleece to size using sharp, fabric-use-only scissors. Remind them that it's better to err on the side of too big at this point. If they make a scarf that is too long or too wide, they can always trim it before sewing it.

## Step 5: Pin Your Fabric

Have kids pin the fabric on the short ends with the pattern on the inside, inserting a pin every 3–4 inches. The fleece that I chose has the same pattern on both sides, so I didn't need to worry about which side faced out.

## Step 6: Sew the Pinned End Together

Have kids use a needle and thread, or a sewing machine, to sew the short ends together.

Figure 3.6 Infinity Scarf

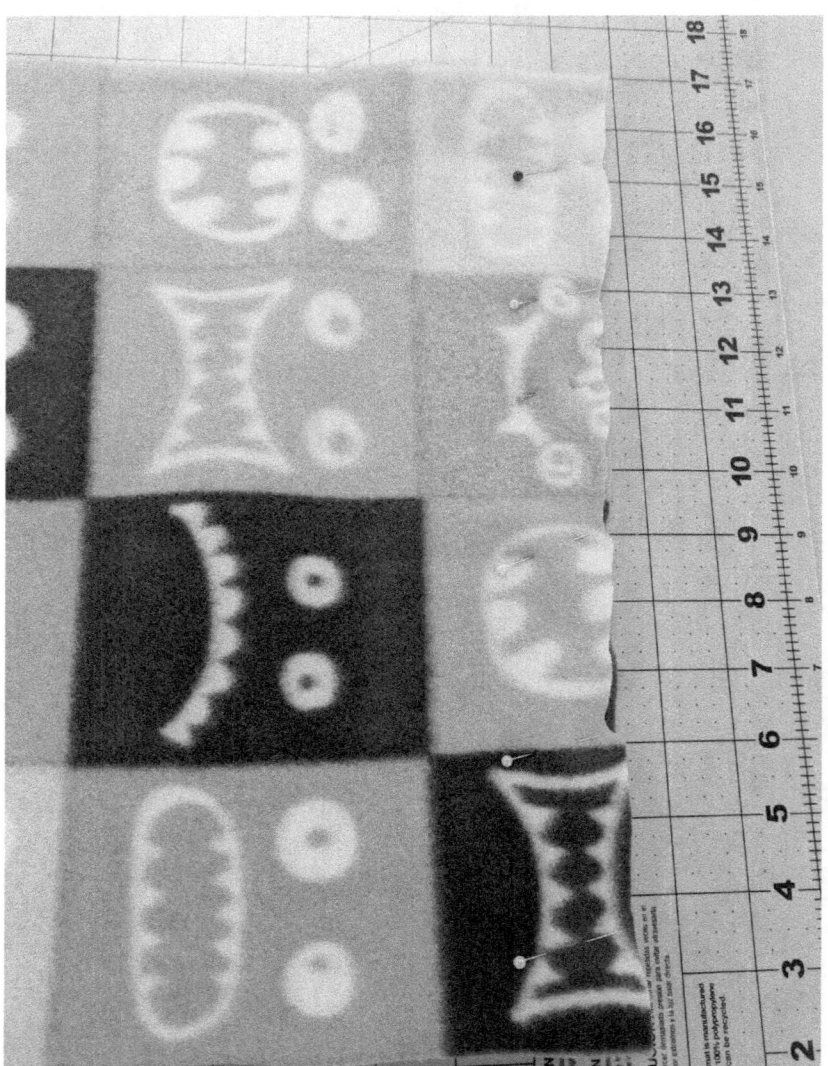

## Step 7: Turn the Fabric So the "Right" Side is Showing

After sewing, have your makers turn their fabric right side out, so that the print is showing on the outside.

## Celebration

As with the classic scarves, make sure that you take photos of someone modeling your lovely neck warmers to post onto social media. Be sure to include positive quotes from the recipients, too. Again, share how many were made and where they were donated. Include any positive feedback from recipients.

Level up the fun by having a fashion show! Map out a "catwalk" and have kids model their completed scarves. You could even invite their grownups to come take photos and watch the show! This could be a stand-alone event or an add-on to a maker-themed night.

Figure 3.7 Infinity Scarf (The completed neck warmers being modeled!)

# Project 3: No-Sew Tie-Pillow Bed for a Shelter Animal

Estimated build time: 1–1 ½ hours.

Learning objectives:

- Students will use measuring tools, fleece fabric, and pillow fill to make a pet bed for a shelter animal.
- Students will make their pet bed according to the shelter-in-need's specifications.
- Students will make a plan to deliver completed pet pillows to the shelter.

Social-Emotional Skills:
  Relationship Skills (CASEL's SEL Framework):

- Students will help others if they complete their projects early (and if others are seeking help).

Social Awareness (CASEL's SEL Framework):

- Students will make pillows to donate to animal shelters, if they have the need. If not, students will consider making pillows as a fundraiser for shelters.

Responsible Decision-Making (CASEL's SEL Framework):

- Students will think through all the steps in this project, and take their time, ensuring that they don't waste materials.

Self-Management (CASEL's SEL Framework):

- Students will manage frustration with tedious tasks, and take a break if needed (there is a lot of knot tying in this project).

Kids love animals. One way that kids love to do good in the world is by helping animals in shelters. These no-sew tie-pillows will allow your makers to give homeless animals some comfort, and feel good about doing some good in the world. This project focuses on empathy, which ties into Social Awareness in CASEL's SEL Framework.

Before introducing this project, contact your local animal shelter so that you can be certain about measurements, and confirm that there's a need, and that donated pet pillows will be accepted. If not, consider making these pet beds as a fundraiser to sell to community members. The proceeds could then go to your local animal shelter, to fulfill their more pressing needs.

## Step 1: Gather Your Materials
What You'll Need

- Sharp scissors (used only with fabric) – 1 per maker
- 1 yard of fleece for each pet bed (more or less will be needed depending on whether the shelter needs beds for kittens, for giant breed dogs, or anything in between).
- Yard stick or quilter's ruler – 1 per work station
- Pencil, chalk, or water erasable fabric pen – 1 per work station
- Pillow fill (enough to fill each bed)

## Step 2: Wash the Fabric
Wash your fabric in advance. Once you create the pet bed, it can be wiped down with a cloth, but it won't survive a washing machine.

## Step 3: Cut Your Fleece
Instruct students to cut two pieces of fleece to the specifications given by the shelter. If they haven't given you guidance, cut these to standard pillow size (20 inches by 26 inches). A standard pillow size will work well for a variety of pets.

## Step 4: Line Up the Top and Bottom of the Pet Bed
Ask kids to lay the two pieces of fleece on top of each other so that the sides all line up. If there is a pattern, have the pattern facing outward.

## Step 5: Measure and Mark Where Your Ties Will Be
Tell your makers to use a yard stick or quilter's ruler to measure a line 2 inches from the edges, on all four sides. Have them use pencil, chalk, water erasable fabric pen (or whatever's on hand) to mark these lines on the fabric.

## Step 6: Cut Out Your Ties
Have kids make cuts, creating a fringe, on all four sides, cutting through both pieces of fleece. Cut to the 2-inch line. Have them make each piece of double fringe about ½–1 inch wide. I usually just have kids eyeball this, but if you're using this project to practice measurement skills, you could have them measure and mark it before cutting. Although I think it's faster to make all the cuts, then go back and tie the pieces together, it's easy to mix up which ties match up when you do it this way. You could also instruct kids to make one cut through both pieces of fabric, tie the fringe together, and then make the next cut.

**Figure 3.8** Tie Pillow
Source: Photo by Terry K. Lawrence

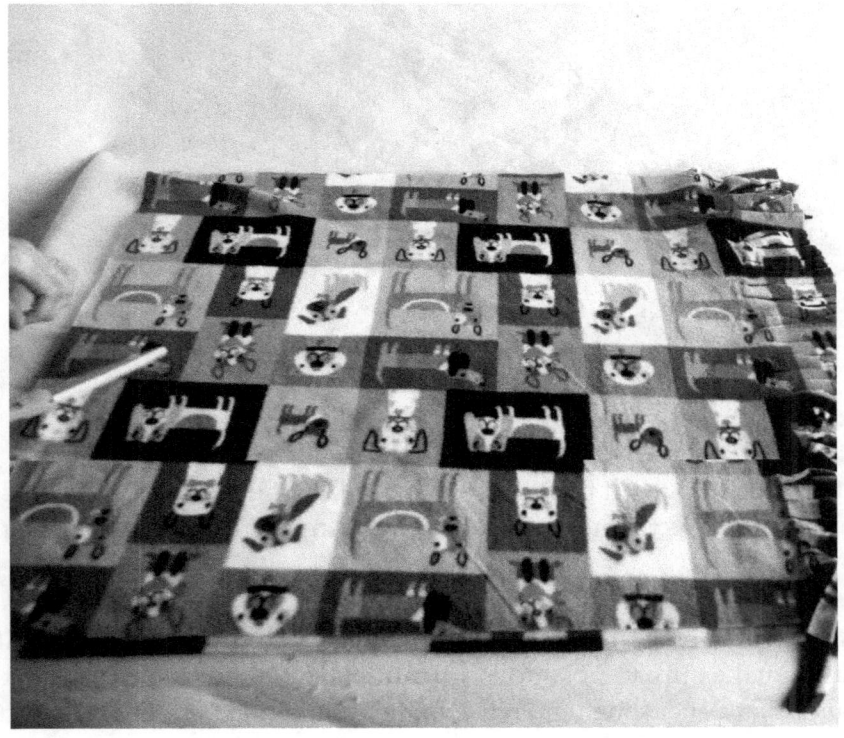

Cutting and tying the fringe is tedious and will be challenging for some kids. Coach kids to be Self-Aware and to think about Self-Management (CASEL's SEL Framework). Have them think through strategies that work for them, when they feel frustrated or overwhelmed by a task, such as taking a short break or taking deep calming breaths. Remind them that perseverance is a powerful skill and that being able to persevere through tasks that are challenging will help them throughout their whole lives.

### Step 7: Tie the Top and the Bottom Fringe Pieces Together

If you're having makers make all of the fringe cuts first, the next task is to have them tie the fringe pieces together (one top fringe to one bottom fringe) using a standard double-knot. Have them tie along all the sides until they have an open gap that's just big enough to fit their hand into.

**Figure 3.9** Tie Pillow
Source: Photo by Terry K. Lawrence

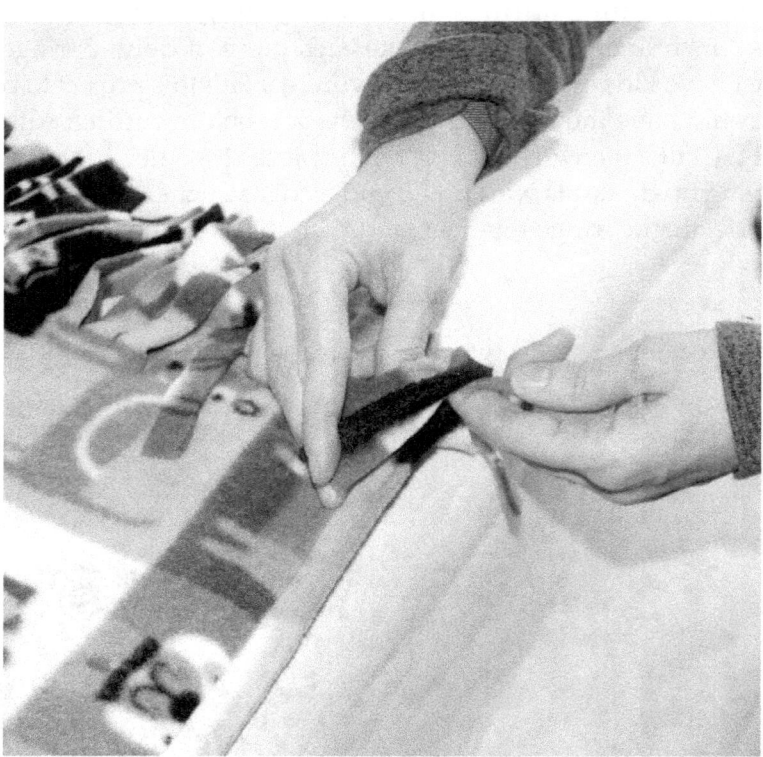

### Step 8: Insert Pillow Fill and Close the Gap

Have them use the open gap to fill their pillow with pillow fill. Once the pillow is fluffy, and the fill is evenly spaced, have them tie the remaining fringe so the fill won't escape.

### Celebration

Take some photos of pets using the pet beds, and post them on social media. If you used this as a fundraiser, make sure to post how much money was earned to support your local animal shelter, and thank everyone who participated in making beds for the fundraiser, and contributed materials.

**Figure 3.10** Tie Pillow
Source: Photo by Terry K. Lawrence

## Conclusion

Textiles are an important part of any makerspace. Use the textiles section of your makerspace to create gifts and donations for your friends, family and community. Start out with fleece, and simple patterns. As your makers gain skill you can move on to using other materials, more complicated patterns, and more sophisticated textile projects.

Projects using textiles are great for developing empathy. Whether you're donating projects to homeless, or animal shelters, thinking about what others need and why they might not have what they need for warmth and comfort helps kids to develop Social Awareness (CASEL's SEL Framework).

# Chapter 4

# Share Our Stories and Learn about Others through Audio and Video Production

Video and audio production are important to makerspace, to give your makers a voice. This can be low-cost using free or inexpensive tools; you can provide them with a professional production studio, or somewhere in between. Video and audio production are extremely engaging and allow you to help kids to develop Self-Awareness when working on their own projects, and Social Awareness and Relationship Skills when viewing or listening to their peers' projects. Kids can also use video and audio production to find an authentic audience beyond their physical space, when it makes sense to do so.

In this chapter, we cover different tools for creating, sharing, and editing videos. We discuss different options for green screens, with detailed instructions on how to create the green screen effect. We also cover podcasting and creating a personalized virtual calming room.

## Projects, Activities, and Resources Included in This Chapter

- Project 1: Make a Video to Share Your Story
- Handout: Movie Storyboard
- Handout: Video Script Starters
- Project 2: Use a Green or Blue Screen to Enhance Your Videos
- Project 3: Use Podcasting to Raise Student Voices
- Handout: Podcast Note Taking
- Handout: Podcast Script Guidelines
- Project 4: Create a Personalized Audio/Visual Virtual Calming Room

## Project 1: Make a Video to Share Your Story

Estimated time: 1–3 hours.

Note: Allowing kids to take longer videos, several videos, and engage in more sophisticated editing and story development (perhaps even making costumes, and using props) will extend this project out even more. This can be a project that takes a few sessions, or it could be an entire elective class, depending upon how you choose to teach it.

DOI: 10.4324/9781003238072-4

Learning objectives:

- Students will develop storyboards and/or scripts before recording videos.
- Students will learn how to complete basic video editing.
- Students will learn to use their videos to share their stories.
- Students will watch their peers' videos, and give supportive, thoughtful feedback.

Social-Emotional Skills:

Relationship Skills (CASEL's SEL Framework):

- Students will work on communicating in positive, supportive ways when giving feedback for videos.

Social Awareness (CASEL's SEL Framework):

- Students will view videos through the lens of thinking about their classmates' perspectives (walking in their shoes).

Responsible Decision-Making (CASEL's SEL Framework):

- Students will think through the steps needed to complete their videos before starting them (including using a storyboard and/or script).

Self-Management (CASEL's SEL Framework):

- Students will make good choices when using equipment.
- Students will share equipment and make certain everyone has equitable time behind the camera (they will need coaching with this and probably a sign-up sheet).
- Students will learn to use their time wisely in order to have time to complete and edit their videos.

Self-Awareness (CASEL's SEL Framework):

- Students will think about the stories that they want to share, and the ways in which they are using their voice, expressing their identity, and sharing their personal experiences.

## Step 1: Decide on Method and Scope, and Gather Your Materials

### What You'll Need

- Video camera and tripod or video camera app. If you have a nice camera with a tripod, you may just have one for the whole group since these are costly, and students will simply have to schedule when they'll record. Having a place where they can sign up for time slots is helpful. If every student has a Chromebook or other device you can opt to use the video camera app, but will need to figure out how to allow them to record without too much ambient noise interference.

- Movie Storyboard Handout (1 per student plus extras for students who may want to storyboard more than 3 scenes)
- Video Script Starters Handout (1 per work station)
- Computers to type up scripts, or paper and pencil to write them by hand (1 per student)

Although you can have kids work in groups (which develops several Social-Emotional Skills), for this project I would encourage you to have all of your makers create their own videos. This will allow them to really dig into the SEL skills related to Self-Awareness such as "Integrating personal and social identities. Identifying personal, cultural, and linguistic assets . . . Linking feelings, values, and thoughts . . . Experiencing self-efficacy" (CASEL's SEL Framework).

Kids can create these videos easily with just a smartphone or a Chromebook. If you want to keep things simple, give your makers three takes, have them pick their favorite of the three, and skip video editing. Video editing is where projects become more sophisticated, but also exponentially more time-consuming. If you want more options, consider the choices below.

### Video Recording and Editing – Free Easy Options

The Chrome extension *Screencastify* is great for quick projects. The only requirement to use it is having Chrome as a browser. With *Screencastify* you can record yourself using your computer's built-in camera, record your computer screen, or both. It also has some basic editing options that kids can use, if they wish to. Additionally, if you create a *Screencastify* account using your Google account, the videos you make will automatically save in a folder called *Screencastify*, in your Google Drive. If you're looking for a quick and easy solution to video production, *Screencastify* is a good option. They even have helpful how-to tutorials on their site for students and teachers (https://www.screencastify.com/courses).

If you want a tool that you can use to have your makers record video and then upload into collated topics, *FlipGrid* could be your best bet. You can also just record yourself in *Zoom*, which you can use with a green screen, too. If you're already familiar and comfortable with one of these tools, that makes it a good choice.

### Video Recording – Options with More Editing Power

However, if you'd like to do more sophisticated video editing, including combining features such as the green screen effect, adding music, titles, transitions, and credits, you'll want something more robust. Since I teach in a lab using Macs, the example I'm using later in this chapter for how to create the green screen effect is *iMovie*. If you want to use cloud-based software, *WeVideo* is also a popular choice. Regardless of which tool you use, start with a writing prompt to keep the focus on sharing stories; this helps kids develop Relationship Skills (CASEL's SEL Framework).

## Step 2: Give Your Makers a Prompt

Give your makers a storytelling prompt to enhance the SEL aspect of this project: sharing our stories and listening to others' stories. Sharing our stories helps us to become more Self-Aware; listening to others' stories allows us to develop Social Awareness and Relationship Skills (CASEL's SEL Framework).

Have your students use this prompt to write out a script. This script can be a page, or several pages, depending upon how much time you have for this project. It should include everything they want to say during the video. Feel free to use the Video Script Starters Handout to help them generate ideas.

## Handout: Video Script Starters

- Who do you admire, and why do you admire that person?
- Talk about a time you witnessed someone do something brave (this someone could be you).
- Talk about something you wish people knew about you.
- What's your wish for the world?
- What's it like to be you; if someone were to walk in your shoes, what would a day in your life be like?
- What are you passionate about?

## Step 3: Have Your Makers Create a Storyboard

Once the script is written out, keep kids focused on their main points by having them use a storyboard to plot out their video scenes. This will also help them plan for props, or other considerations.

If kids don't know what a storyboard is, it's useful to compare it to a graphic novel. If your makers don't enjoy drawing, but still prefer the storyboard style of planning, you can have them use a site such as *Make Beliefs Comix*, where the characters and props are supplied, and they can click and drag them online to populate a storyboard (and then print or email it). If your makers want to hand-draw, use the handout provided on the next page.

## Handout: Movie Storyboard

Use the boxes below to plan your movie. Use drawings (in the top boxes) and words (in the bottom boxes) to show what will happen in each scene. Use additional pages if needed.

## Step 4: Recording and Considerations for Leveling Up

Once the script and storyboard are complete, it's time for makers to record their videos. Although (as mentioned) students could do this with a video camera, tablet, Chromebook, or smartphone, the best choice for features and quality, especially if you can stick to a schedule, is a video camera with a tripod, used in a devoted space. Not only does this give your makers more options while filming, but it makes using the green screen a lot easier. It's difficult to line up shots when you're trying to aim a computer camera, and hard to keep a phone camera steady, and properly aimed, when it's in your hand. If you'd like to keep things simple, skip the next part and jump to Step 5. If you want some ideas for leveling up your video production, continue on.

If you have a large budget, and you're using a handheld device, or you just want more options for moving around, you could consider using a stabilizer rig. You can find them for video camcorders, *GoPros*, and phones; there are even body harness stabilizer rigs. You could also consider something like *Swivl*. *Swivl* is a device that follows your movements around a space, while you're recording video. The videos can then be uploaded for review, and commentary.

Think about sound quality in the space that you'll use for recording. For good quality videos, students need a space devoid of too much ambient noise. We use a room adjacent to the library which we call "The Green Screen Room" for recording our videos (with the door propped open a little, so I can still keep an eye on our makers).

Perhaps you don't have a devoted space available. If you're handy, you can make one. I asked Acoustical Engineer Andrea Frey if a large cardboard box (such as an empty refrigerator box) could work. This was her advice:

> The two concepts at work here [in creating a soundproof space] are sound transmission loss – STL – (keeping unwanted sound out) and sound absorption (reducing echo inside the space).
>
> STL depends mainly on mass and not having any holes. So cardboard would work, but thin particle board would work better, and thick particle board would work even better. And then you'd just have to make sure you seal all the joints with caulk or something.
>
> For absorption, you can line it on the inside with the egg-crate foam that you can buy at guitar stores.

If building a recording room seems daunting, recording in something like a coat closet also actually works surprisingly well (obviously this would be better for audio than video), since clothing is good for sound absorption. In this same vein, a carpeted area is better than a room with a hard floor.

Although the built-in microphone that you have on whatever device you're using may work just fine, there are some situations where you may want to invest in a better-quality microphone. Purchasing a *Snowball* microphone can vastly improve your sound and you can find a good quality one for under $100.

## Step 5: Transferring Your Videos

Transferring videos from phones to computers, for editing, can pose challenges, due to issues such as slow Internet. Videos are large files that can take a lot of time to upload. Length and quality will both impact how big video files are (and consequently how long they take to upload). My high-quality videos that are close to an hour in length take me several hours to upload to YouTube.

Fortunately, kids are usually working with short video clips. This makes everything much faster and easier. Also, if they're using the same device to record, edit, and upload, some of these issues can be circumvented.

When using a video camera, you can remove the SD (Secure Digital) card from the camera and insert it into an SD card reader (or sometimes directly into a computer). From there, drag and drop the video files from the SD card to the computer's desktop, where kids can work on editing the files. I would recommend purchasing an SD card reader that supports several different sizes and shapes of SD/SDHC (Secure Digital High Capacity) cards. You can usually find a decent one for around $10.

### Step 6: Share Your Videos

Many educators pair video recording with the digital portfolio software *Seesaw*. Using *Seesaw*, kids take videos of schoolwork, events, or other related topics, and send them directly to their grownups at home. Home access to *Seesaw* is obtained through a link that is sent directly from the teacher, so the kid's personal information, as shared through these videos, has some protection.

You can also create your own channel on YouTube for kids' videos. Once a video is uploaded, click "edit," and then choose the "unlisted" option. Doing this keeps the videos from being public or searchable. To share with others, you will need to provide them with the direct link to these videos.

If you're recording on a site such as *FlipGrid*, sharing onto your *FlipGrid* teacher site is already built into the recording and saving process.

Whatever option you choose for sharing, just make sure your makers aren't sharing any personal information in a space where everyone can see it. Safety should always be the first consideration when students share videos. Having kids think about safety also helps them to develop skills related to Responsible Decision-Making (CASEL's SEL Framework).

### Celebration

To celebrate your video projects, and incorporate SEL skills, host a film festival. This could be in person, virtual, or both. This could be done with just your kids, or you could invite their grownups to view the completed videos.

If you want to make this more low-key, you could also have your makers share their videos with each other, in a small group setting. After the video is shared, encourage them to connect by having viewers share something they learned about the video producer, or something they really enjoyed about the video (this ties in Relationship Skills). If you include time for them to talk about their process, this will also help them to develop Self-Awareness (CASEL's SEL Framework).

## Project 2: Use a Green or Blue Screen to Enhance Your Videos

Estimated time: 1–2 hours.

Learning objectives:

- Students will learn how to use a blue or green screen to create a virtual background.
- Students will choose background images that enhance the message of their videos.

Social-Emotional Skills:
Relationship Skills (CASEL's SEL Framework):

- Students will effectively communicate when using shared equipment such as green screens.

Social Awareness (CASEL's SEL Framework):

- Students will make sure their videos and images are appropriate and culturally sensitive.

Responsible Decision-Making (CASEL's SEL Framework):

- Students will take time to think through which images would best match up with their videos and send the message they intend.

Self-Management (CASEL's SEL Framework):

- Students will make good choices with school-appropriate background images that convey the message they are trying to send with their videos.

Self-Awareness (CASEL's SEL Framework):

- Students can really explore their interests, thoughts, and feelings through the use of a green screen. Figuring out a background to match up with their videos is a great way to develop Self-Awareness through creative exploration.

## Step 1: In Advance – Purchase or Make Your Green or Blue Screen

Green and blue screens are backgrounds, made out of fabric or paint, in a very specific shade of green or blue (sometimes called chroma key). These two colors – blue and green – are the furthest away, on the color spectrum, from skin tones. This means that a blue or green background can be replaced by an image or video, using a computer, without that image or video blending into the person, by mistake. However, blue screens can sometimes be problematic if you are filming people with blue eyes, so green screens are more widely used.

Common users of green screens are newscasters to show weather patterns, and more recently office workers as a personal background for meetings using Zoom. My makers use them for all sorts of things. Recently, a group created a music video with backgrounds that looked like they were traveling all over the world. Sometimes my makers purposely wear green T-shirts so that they look like they have floating heads, because they think it's funny (they're right, it is).

Our green screen is a big piece of green material, on posts that are pretty much like tent poles. We purchased it on Amazon. However, you can make your own green screen using

PVC pipe and green cloth. It helps to have a sewing machine, too, so you can sew the top of the cloth, so that it slides over the PVC pipe on which it hangs. If you want to keep it really simple, and you have a smooth available wall (or large piece of foam), you can also just paint the wall, or piece of foam, chroma key green. You can even buy pre-painted chroma key green foam pieces. Special chroma key green paint is expensive, so if you don't want to shell out the cash for the official stuff, you could also just purchase a bright green paint that matches up pretty closely.

### Step 2: Record Your Videos in Front of Your Green Screen

When kids take videos in front of a green screen, have them work to limit any wrinkles or shadows in their camera shot. The background of their video recording should be entirely taken up by the green screen. Any corners that show outside of the green screen will mess up the green screen effect.

### Step 3: Select and Download Background Image(s)

After your makers have taken some good videos in front of the green or blue screen, a background image needs to be chosen. I usually have students take a photo or download something off the Internet, respecting copyright law of course. Use of background images or videos created by other people, which are used for *learning about video production*, may be covered under the fair use copyright law. Fair use allows the limited use of some content, created by other people, as long as credit is given, and the use of this content is *exclusively for educational purposes*. There are strict limits on the amount of content that can be used, as well as limits on the ways in which it can be used. Most certified librarians or media specialists can help to explain the details. Just make sure that your makers don't upload the completed videos, using content created by other people, onto any other online sites such as social media sites. At that point, it's likely a copyright violation.

Another way to respect copyright is to get permission from the artist who created the work. If permission is given, make sure that it's in writing and that you hang onto it (email is fine). Your makers can also use stock photos or works in the public domain. A great site with beautiful, free-to-use photos is *unsplash.com*; just don't forget to have kids give credit to the photographer in their bibliography. If you want to err on the safe side, you can also just create everything from scratch, including background images. Then there's no need to worry. If you go this route, these could be shared on social media without violating copyright (although you still might discourage this, due to safety concerns).

Once you have your videos, and background images, it's time to put them together. I'm going to show you how to do this with *iMovie*, but it translates to other software, too. In most video editing software, you are working with three panels: preview panes where you can see a preview of what your video looks like, the media library which includes all of the content that you've uploaded to the video editing software, and the timeline where you are doing most of the editing. Here's how it works in *iMovie*.

### Step 4: Using *iMovie* – Create a New Movie File

Have kids open up *iMovie* and create a new movie file by clicking on "Create New."

Tell them to select the *Movie* option, *not* the Trailer. The trailer is really cool; it makes a professional-looking movie from a template, but it will be trickier to use the green screen effect in a trailer.

Use Multimedia to Share Our Stories 73

Figure 4.1 Green Screen

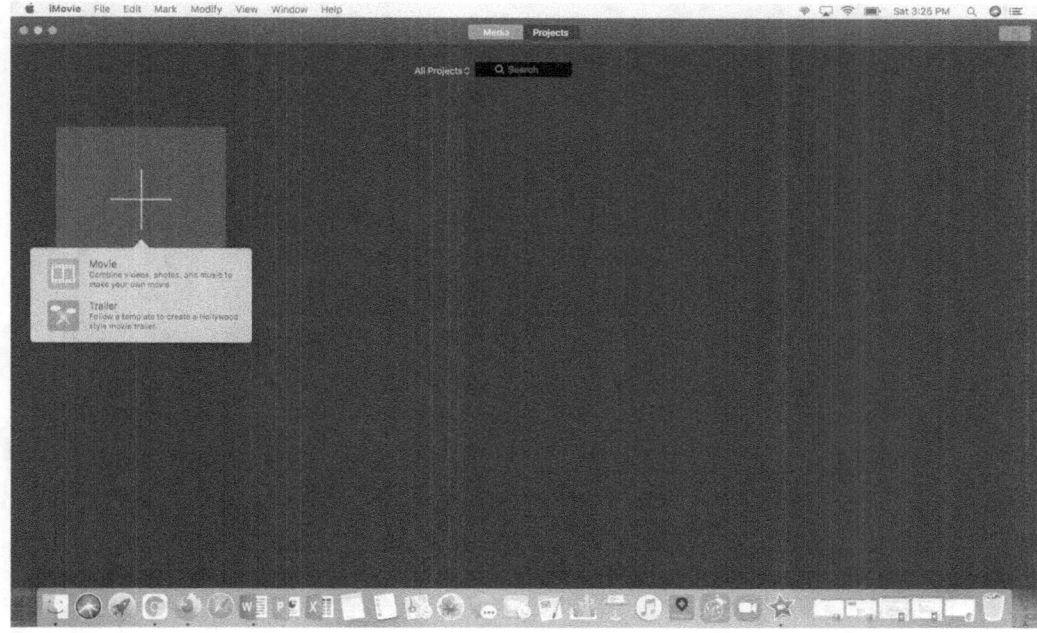

## Step 5: Import Video Footage and Background Images
Have kids import their video footage and background images by clicking on "Import Media."
 Have them select their video and image files, and then click on "Import Selected."
 Note: If the files are grayed out when they're trying to select media, these files are likely not in a format that works with *iMovie* and will need to be converted in order to use them with *iMovie*. I usually use .jpg and .mp4 files when I'm working with *iMovie*.

Figure 4.2 Green Screen

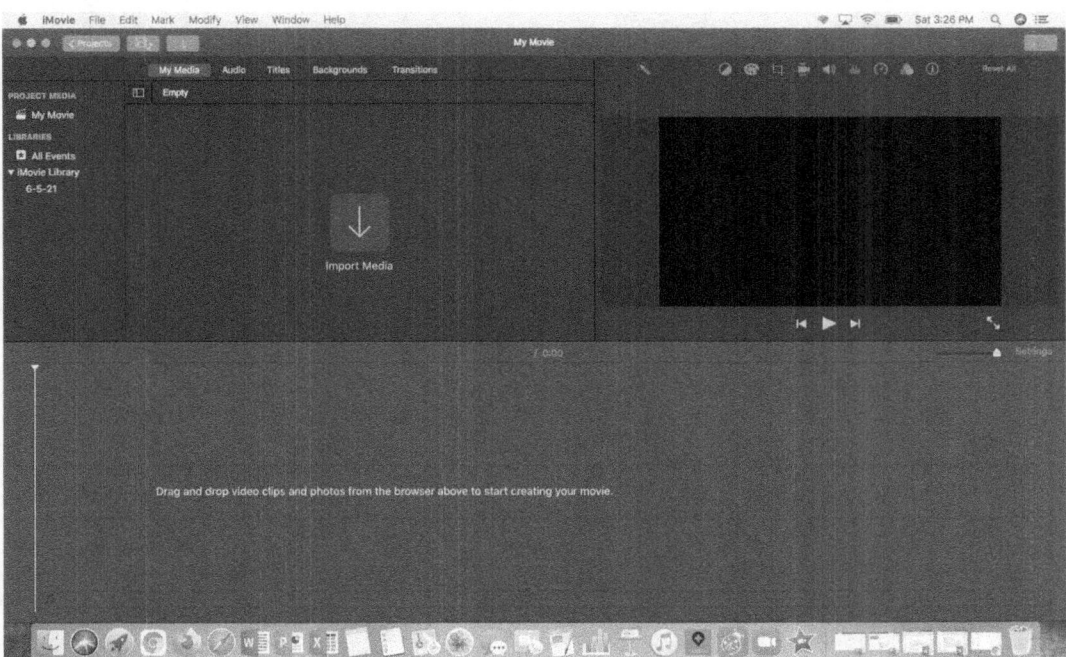

74    Use Multimedia to Share Our Stories

Figure 4.3 Green Screen

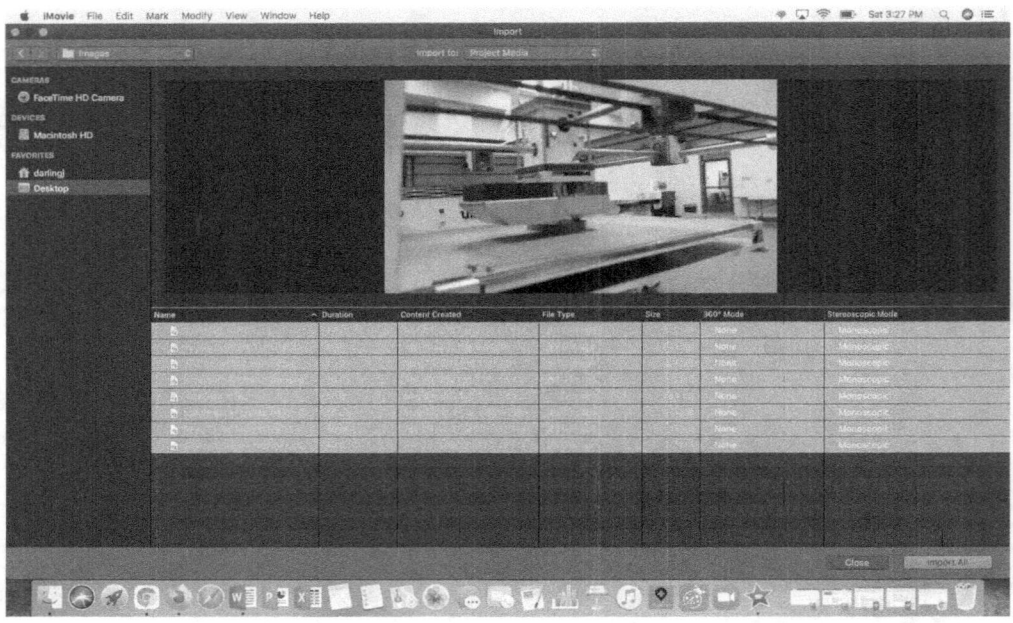

## Step 6: Put Your Files into Your Timeline

Your makers will need to get both the video and image file into their timeline in order to apply the green screen effect. Have them click once to select the file, and then click the plus sign in the lower right-hand corner to add it to their timeline.

Note: When they've selected both their video and their background image, and put them into their timeline (following the steps above), these files will initially appear in their timeline side by side.

Figure 4.4 Green Screen

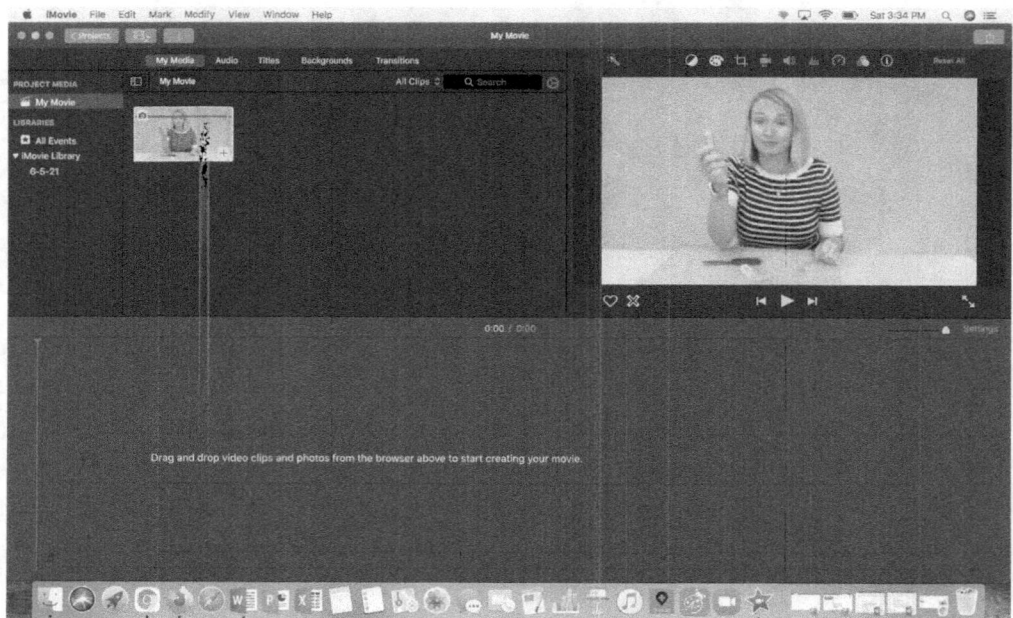

Figure 4.5 Green Screen

## Step 7: Drag Video File(s) on Top of Background Image(s)

Have your makers click and drag their *video* file *on top of* their background image. The video has to go *above* the image, or the green screen effect won't work.

Note: Most likely the image will initially appear for less time in the timeline than the video. If your makers want an image to be displayed for the entire length of the video, they can fix this; click and drag the image from the right side until it displays for the same length of time as their video clip. (They can also put different images in the background throughout their video clip.) Exploring which images to choose and how long they're displayed helps kids to develop video production editing skills and explore Self-Awareness through exploration and perhaps even "linking feelings, values and thoughts" (CASEL's SEL Framework).

Figure 4.6 Green Screen

## Step 8: Click to View Video Overlay Settings

Have kids click above any point on their timeline to select it, and they'll see two squares on top of each other appear on the far left side of the preview panel (which is on the top right side of the screen). This is the Video Overlay Settings button.

Figure 4.7 Green Screen

## Step 9: Select the Blue/Green Screen Button

Have kids click on the video overlay settings button and a drop-down menu will appear. Next, have them select the Blue/Green Screen Option from this drop-down.

They'll see in the preview panel that their image is the new background for their video, and has replaced the green screen.

Figure 4.8 Green Screen

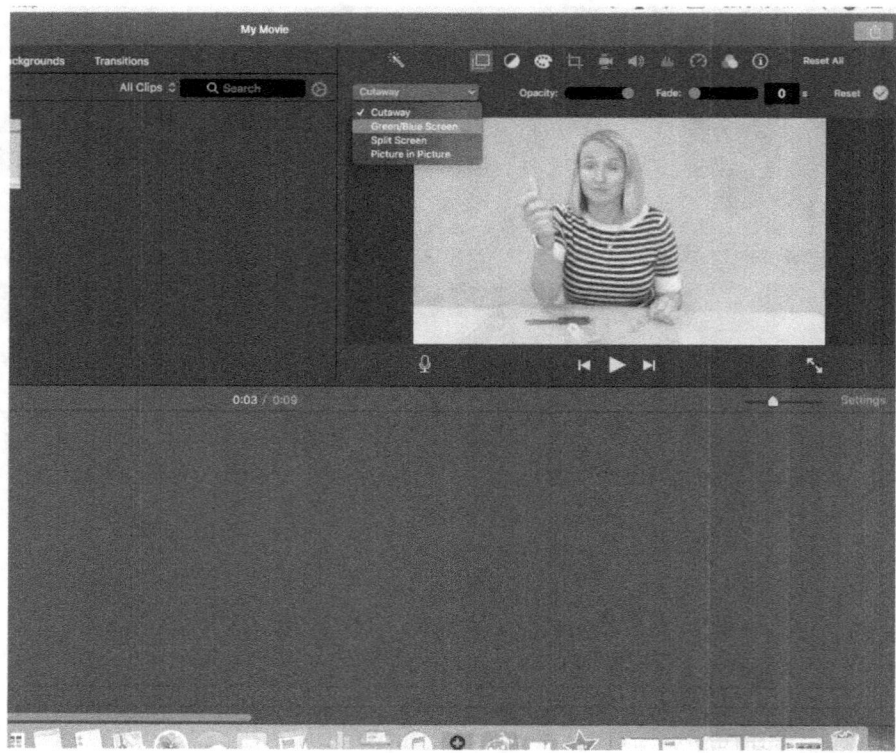

Figure 4.9 Green Screen

## Step 10: Export Your Completed Video

Once the video is finished, kids can export their completed video back to their desktop by clicking on the "Share" arrow in the top right corner of their *iMovie* screen, and selecting "File."

Figure 4.10 Green Screen

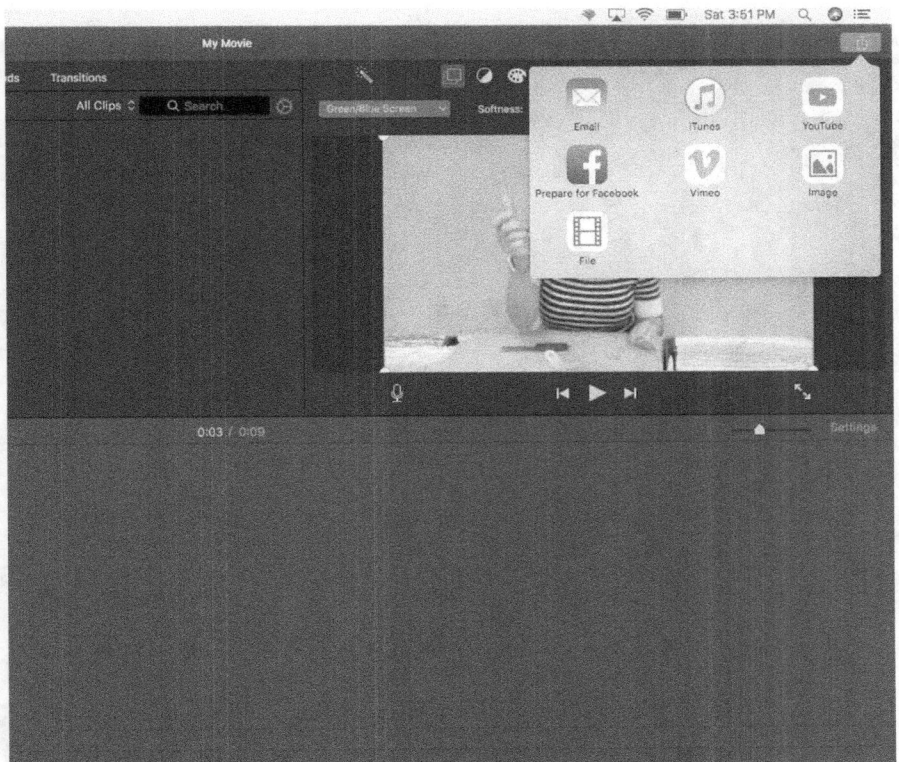

78  Use Multimedia to Share Our Stories

Note: Although you can export from *iMovie* directly to YouTube, I find that often requires some troubleshooting. Directing kids to share their movie as a file to their desktop first usually works better.

I tell kids to leave the default settings, and click "Next" to get the option to save the video to their desktop, so it's easy to find when they're ready to upload it.

They'll get a pop-up notification when the export has been successfully saved.

From their desktop, they can upload the completed movie to storage space in the cloud, YouTube, or whatever you prefer. If you opt for YouTube, use an unlisted channel in YouTube for safety. When recording videos, I also instruct students to use secret code names, instead of their real names.

Figure 4.11 Green Screen

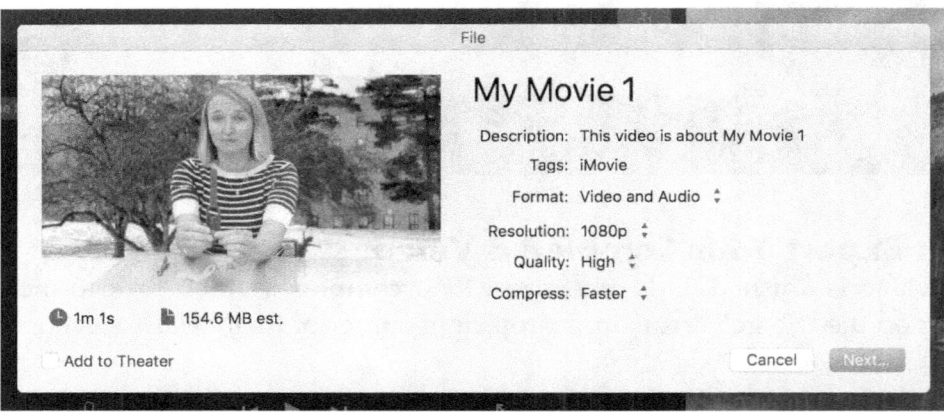

Figure 4.12 Green Screen

## Celebration

A movie festival of some sort is the best celebration when working with movie production. Have students talk through which background they chose, and why they chose their topic. Articulating this gives them another avenue through which to explore Self-Awareness.

## Project 3: Use Podcasting to Raise Student Voices

Estimated time: 1 ½–2 hours.

Learning objectives:

- Students will listen to a podcast to develop an understanding about how they work.
- Students will write out a script to keep their podcast focused.
- Students will learn how to use recording software to record and share their podcast.

Social-Emotional Skills:

Relationship Skills (CASEL's SEL Framework):

- Students will listen to each other's podcasts and provide supportive feedback.

Social Awareness (CASEL's SEL Framework):

- Students will consider the message their peers are sending with their podcasts, and think about others' feelings and experiences.
- Students will consider the message they're sending with their podcast and think about how that message could impact others.

Responsible Decision-Making (CASEL's SEL Framework):

- Students will think through the steps for creating a podcast, before recording.

Self-Management (CASEL's SEL Framework):

- Students will make good choices and take turns when using recording equipment.

Self-Awareness (CASEL's SEL Framework):

- Students will develop a podcast about an issue they care about, through an examination of their own experiences, passions, and values.

## Step 1: Gather Your Materials

### What You'll Need

- A computer or device for each student or pair of students to use to record their podcasts
- A quiet space that students can use to record their podcasts
- Copies of the Podcast Note Taking Handout for all students
- Copies of the Podcast Script Guidelines Handout for all students
- Paper and pencil or access to a computer for students to use to write out their podcast scripts

Although kids love creating videos, there is one major advantage to guiding them toward podcasts (just audio, no video) instead – it's much easier to keep their identities safe with a podcast (compared with a video). Podcasts can be incredibly engaging, and you can teach kids to keep all identifying information out of the podcast. This can be a good way to have kids share news about your organization. It's also a great way for them to talk about topics that they care about, which helps them to develop Self-Awareness. Listening to each other's podcasts encourages Social Awareness.

## Step 2: Have Students Listen to a Podcast and Take Notes

Many of my students don't know what a podcast is; some listen to podcasts with their grownups; and a few listen on their own. Before they develop their own podcast, it's a good idea to have them listen to one (or more than one). Here are some kid-friendly choices:

- Short & Curly: https://www.abc.net.au/radio/programs/shortandcurly/
- But Why: https://www.npr.org/podcasts/474377890/but-why-a-podcast-for-curious-kids
- Wow in the World: https://www.npr.org/podcasts/510321/wow-in-the-world
- The Chat with Mrs. Burns's 3rd Grade: https://audioboom.com/channels/4925886

While students are listening to their podcasts, have them take some notes. The Podcast Note Taking Handout can help them stay focused. Asking kids why they chose that particular podcast also helps them with Self-Awareness (thinking about their own choices and preferences).

# Handout: Podcast Note Taking

What is the title of the podcast you chose to listen to?

What made you choose this one?

What made this podcast interesting to listen to?

Did the host(s) seem passionate about the topic? If so, how could you tell?

What did this podcast teach you?

## Step 3: Write a Script

Next, have students write out a script of exactly what they plan to say during their podcast. Make sure they add information about techniques they plan to use in order to grab and keep the audience's attention. Will they use sound effects? Different voices? Is there going to be something unexpected in the story, or some sort of plot twist? Will they reflect on a lesson learned or include a teaser at the beginning that makes their audience want to know what's going to happen next? Ask them to think about the podcast(s) that they listened to and identify any engaging techniques that were used, that they'd like to include in theirs. Use the Podcast Script Guidelines Handout to help them stay focused.

## Handout: Podcast Script Guidelines

Use these guidelines to write your podcast script. Your script should include everything you intend to say in the recording and notes about any techniques you plan to use to engage your audience. Make sure to label your script with these same headings: Engaging Techniques, Beginning, Middle, and End.

### Engaging Techniques
Which engaging storytelling techniques will you use in your podcast? Sound effects? Different Voices?

### Beginning
How will you start your podcast? Will you include a teaser that makes your audience want to know what happens? For example, "When I woke up this morning, I had no idea that today . . . my life would change forever."

### Middle
This is the main content of your podcast. What are some important details that shouldn't be forgotten? What do you want the main takeaway(s) to be?

### End
How will you end your podcast? Will there be a dramatic plot twist? Will you reflect on a lesson learned?

84    Use Multimedia to Share Our Stories

### Step 4: Record the Podcast

If you wanted to really dig into editing sound, you could record or import your recording into Audacity: https://www.audacityteam.org/. Audacity is a free, open-source, downloadable program that gives you lots of powerful editing tools. However, it's not super-intuitive. Using Audacity gives you more control, but will also add more time to this project. If you're working with littler kids, or if you'd just prefer to keep it simple, use cloud-based Vocaroo (https://vocaroo.com/) instead. Not only can you record your podcast in just two clicks in Vocaroo, but when you save the recording, Vocaroo creates a link to use to share your podcast, too.

### Step 5: Share the Podcast

Once you have your audio file, you can share it by posting it to your organization's website, through your preferred learning management system, on social media, or through an official podcast hosting site. If you want to make it an official podcast that others can subscribe to, you can use a site like Anchor: https://anchor.fm/ to help you distribute it to Spotify or Apple Podcasts.

### Celebration

Celebrate your makers' incredible audio content through a listening party. Listening parties could be a shared event where kids listen to each other's podcasts and tell each other something they liked and learned, from listening. This helps them to develop both Social Awareness and Relationship Skills.

## Project 4: Create a Personalized Audio/ Visual Virtual Calming Room

Estimated time: 1 ½–2 hours.

Learning objectives:

- ♦ Students will create a virtual calming room to use when they need a break.
- ♦ Students will learn how to create a Google Slideshow.
- ♦ Students will learn how to upload and download images and sounds for use in their calming room.

Social-Emotional Skills:

Responsible Decision-Making (CASEL's SEL Framework):

- ♦ Students will give credit to images and sounds made by others.

Self-Management (CASEL's SEL Framework):

- ♦ Students will think about scenarios where using a virtual calming room can help make them feel more grounded and positive.

Self-Awareness (CASEL's SEL Framework):

♦ Students will analyze and select visual and audio elements that make them feel calm, to use for their calming room.

This project really digs into Self-Awareness. It helps students to think through how they feel when they're stressed out or feeling any other strong, negative emotion, and provides an option for how to self-soothe, namely by enjoying their very own personalized virtual calming room.

To complete this project, students will need access to a computer, with Internet access and a G Suite (Google Workspace) account. Headphones or earbuds are also useful for when they're exploring sounds to add to their calming rooms, especially if they're working in a classroom setting. It's also helpful for them to keep the following tabs open, once they've navigated there: their Google Drive, the Google Slideshow that they will create, the site with free images (unsplash.com), and the site with free sounds (http://dig.ccmixter.org/). That way, if they need to go back for any reason, they won't have to search for everything all over again. Any additional tabs should be closed while working on this project.

## Step 1: Familiarize Yourself with Virtual Calming Rooms

Start by familiarizing students with what a visual virtual calming room looks like, so they can get some ideas for how theirs might look. Have them Google "Virtual Calming Room" or go to this example: https://calmingroom.scusd.edu/. Make sure they understand that they will be creating their own by pairing a soothing sound with an image.

## Step 2: Create a Google Slideshow with 3 Slides

Instruct students to create the slideshow in their Google Drive. Tell them to open up their Google Drive and click on "New."

Next, have them mouse down and click on "Google Slides."

Figure 4.13 Virtual Calming Room

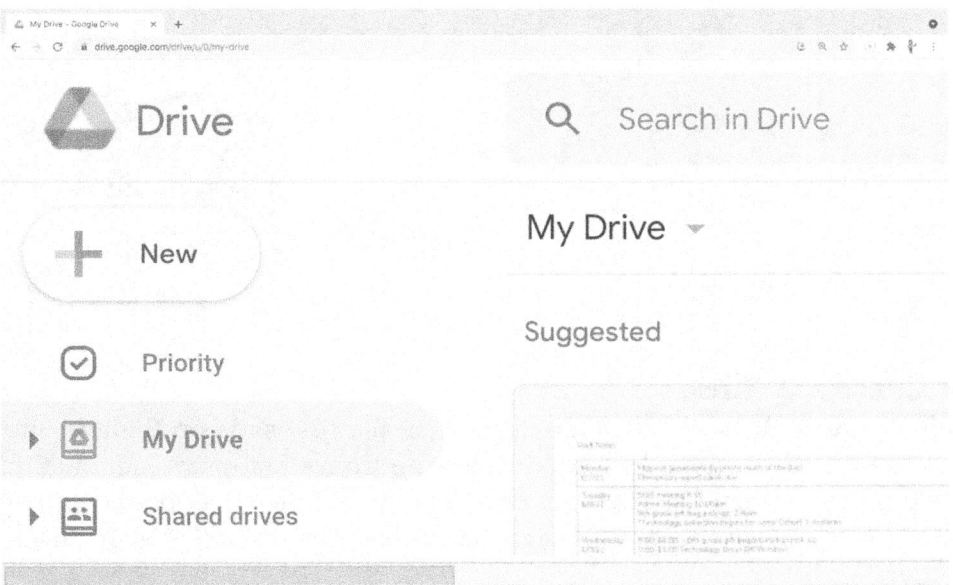

86   Use Multimedia to Share Our Stories

Figure 4.14 Virtual Calming Room

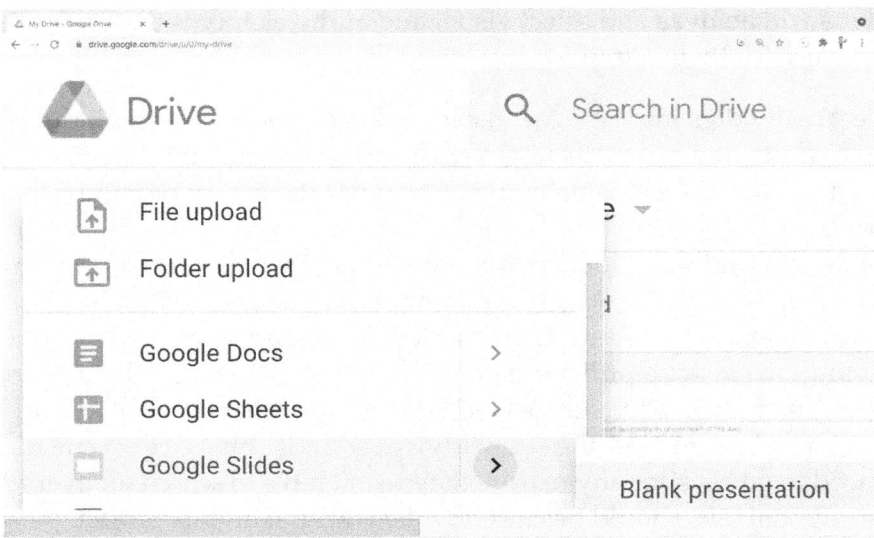

## Step 3: Name the Slideshow
Have students click in the top left-hand corner where it says "Untitled presentation" and click once in that box – have them name their slideshow "Virtual Calming Room – [Your Name]." For example, mine would be called: Virtual Calming Room – Julie Darling.

Figure 4.15 Virtual Calming Room

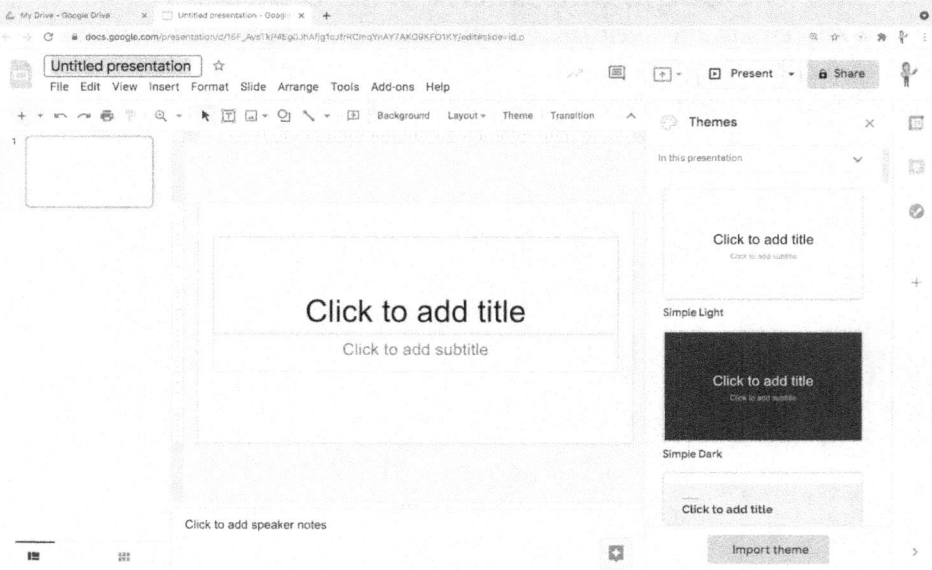

## Step 4: Create 3 Slides
Have students create 3 slides by either clicking on the first slide on the left, and pressing Return/Enter on their keyboard twice, or selecting from the top navigation: Slide > New slide. Note that the keyboard shortcut for creating a new slide will appear to the right of this drop-down navigation (in this case, it says that the shortcut is Ctrl + M or the Control key plus the letter "M").

Figure 4.16 Virtual Calming Room

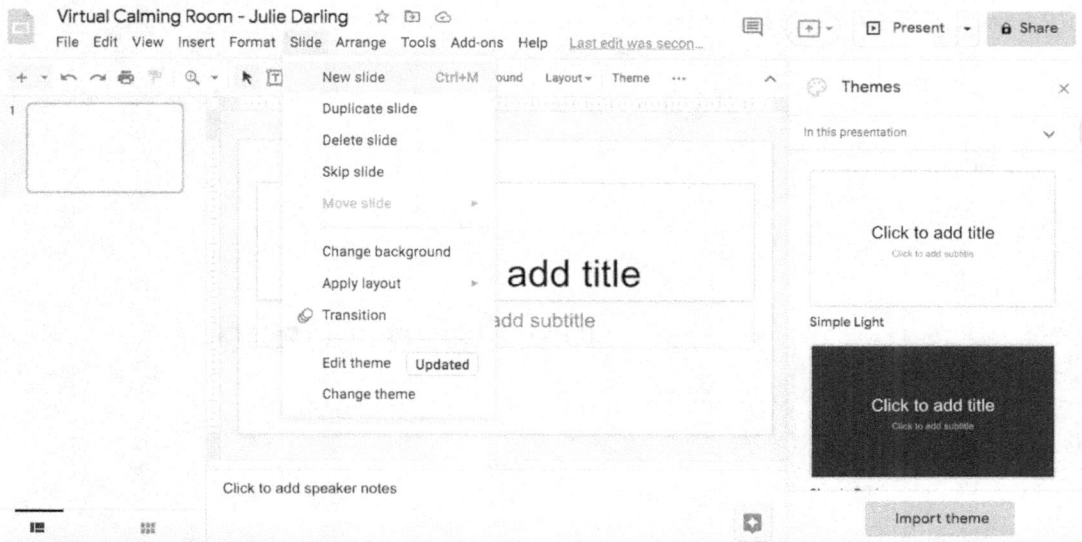

## Step 5: Label the Slides

Next, students should click on the left-hand side to select the first slide, then click in the box in the middle where it says, "Click to add title."

Have them type in their calming room title. Next, have them click in the box that says, "Click to add subtitle" and have them type in their name.

Next, instruct them to click to select their 3rd slide (the one with the 3 next to it on the left).

Then click in the box in the middle where it says, "Click to add title" and type "Bibliography."

Figure 4.17 Virtual Calming Room

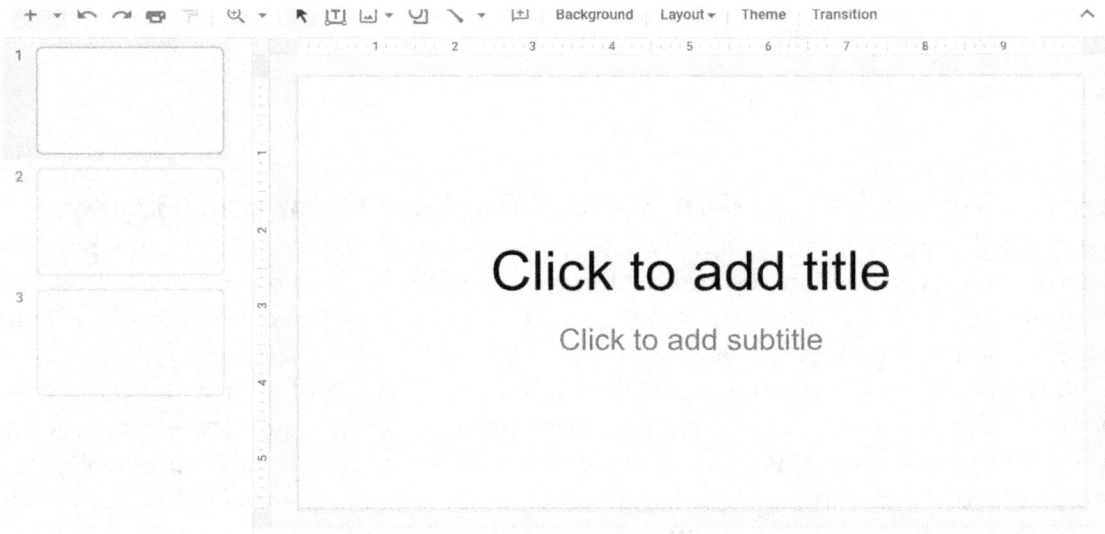

88   Use Multimedia to Share Our Stories

Figure 4.18 Virtual Calming Room

Figure 4.19 Virtual Calming Room

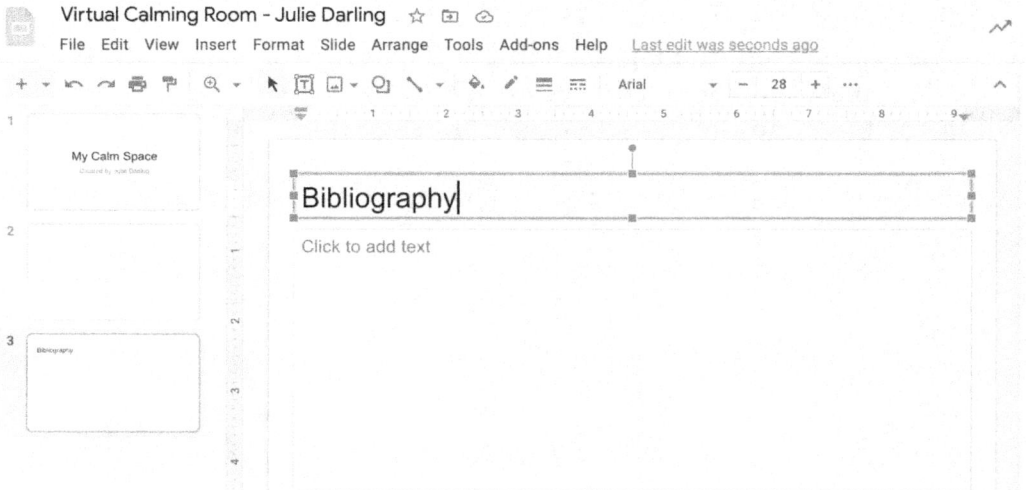

## Step 6: Find an Image that Makes You Feel Calm and Happy

Have students search for an image by going to a website with free images; unsplash.com is a good choice as these images are free for anyone to use as long as you give credit to the photographer. Have them start by clicking in the top search bar box, where it says, "Search free high-resolution photos."

Tell them to type in something that makes them feel calm and happy and press Enter/Return on their keyboard. Some ideas for search terms are ocean, mountains, or trees. Once they find an image they'd like to use, have them mouse over the image and click on the download arrow in the lower right-hand corner. This will save the image for them in their downloads folder.

Figure 4.20 Virtual Calming Room

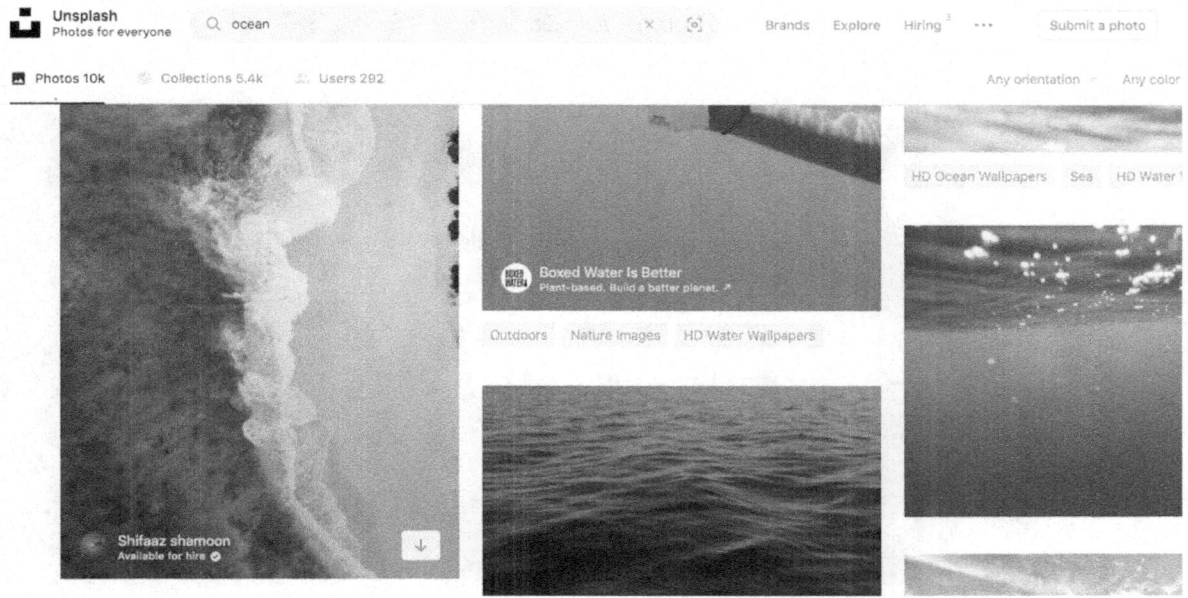

## Step 7: Copy Citation Information for Use of the Image
A "Say thanks" box will pop up with information about giving credit. Tell students to click on the overlapping boxes in the lower right-hand corner to copy this information (so that they can give credit in the bibliography section of their slideshow).

Figure 4.21 Virtual Calming Room

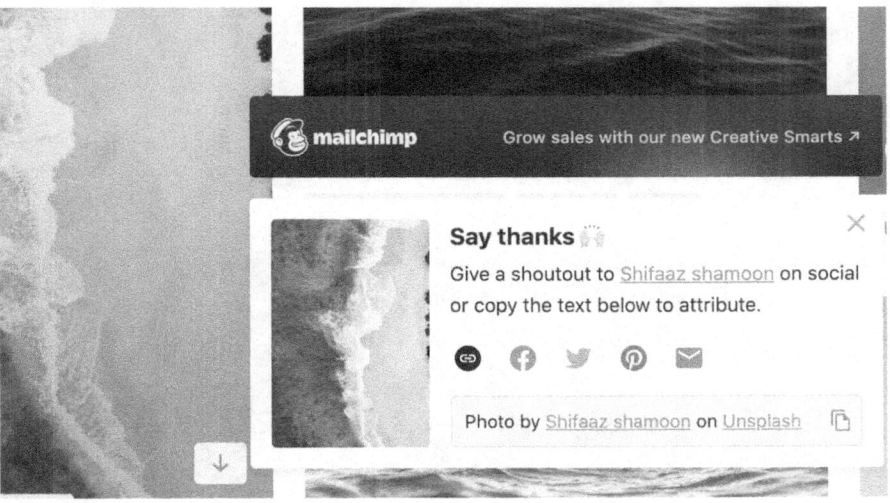

## Step 8: Paste Citation Information into the 3rd Google Slide
Have kids head back over to their virtual calming room slides and paste the photo credit information (on a PC such as a Chromebook the shortcut is Control + V to paste; on a Mac it's Command + V) into the 3rd slide, in the larger, bottom box – the one that they titled "Bibliography."

Figure 4.22 Virtual Calming Room

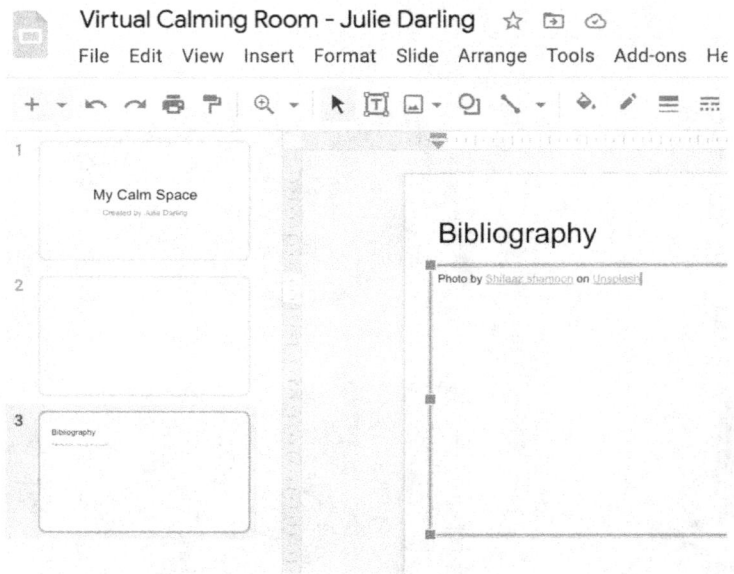

## Step 9: Select the 2nd Slide and Get Ready to Insert the Image

Have kids click in the 2nd box of their Google Slideshow, on the left-hand side.

Note: Make sure it's the smaller slide on the far left-hand side; if they click on the large editable slide in the middle they won't see the "Background" option, which is what they need for the next step.

Figure 4.23 Virtual Calming Room

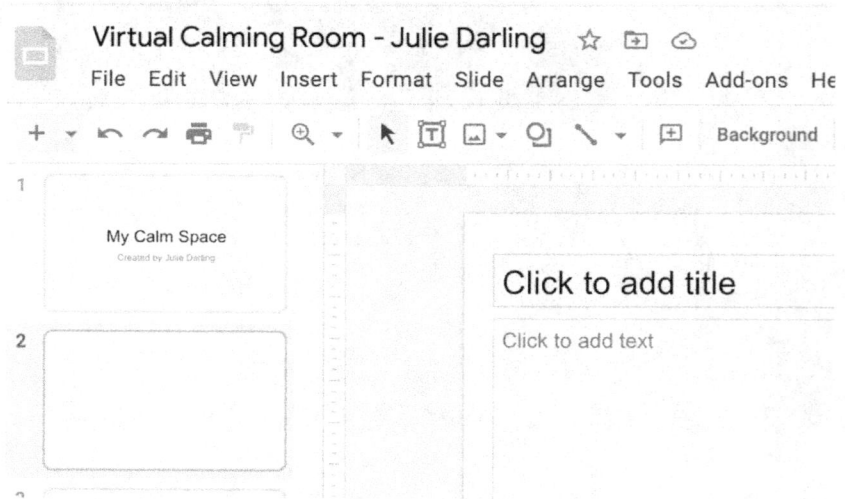

## Step 10: Select "Background"

Have kids click on the word "Background" in the top middle bar. A box should pop up that looks like this:

Use Multimedia to Share Our Stories    91

Figure 4.24 Virtual Calming Room

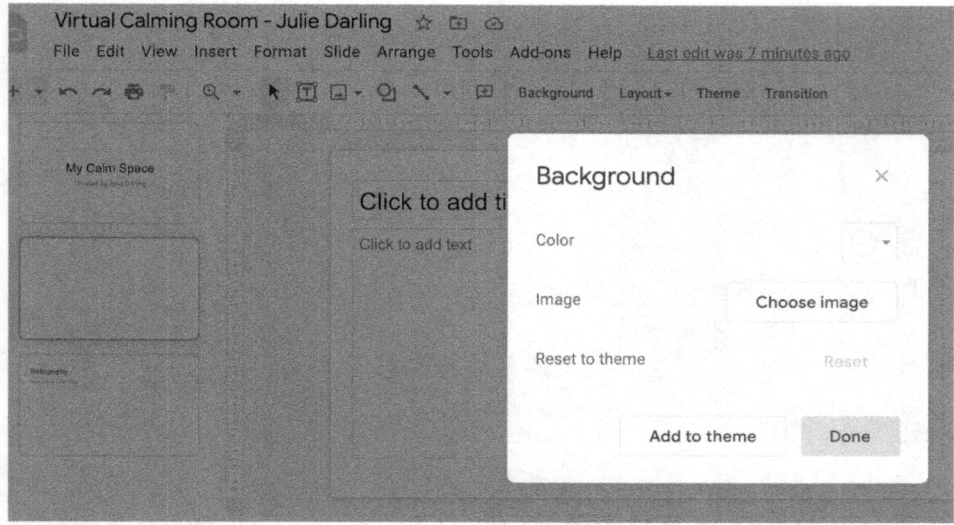

## Step 11: Select and Insert Your Image as the Background of Your 2nd Slide

Ask kids to click on the "Choose image" box, find and select their image (it should be in their "Downloads" folder), "Browse" for it (make sure they're looking in their Downloads folder for it).

Figure 4.25 Virtual Calming Room

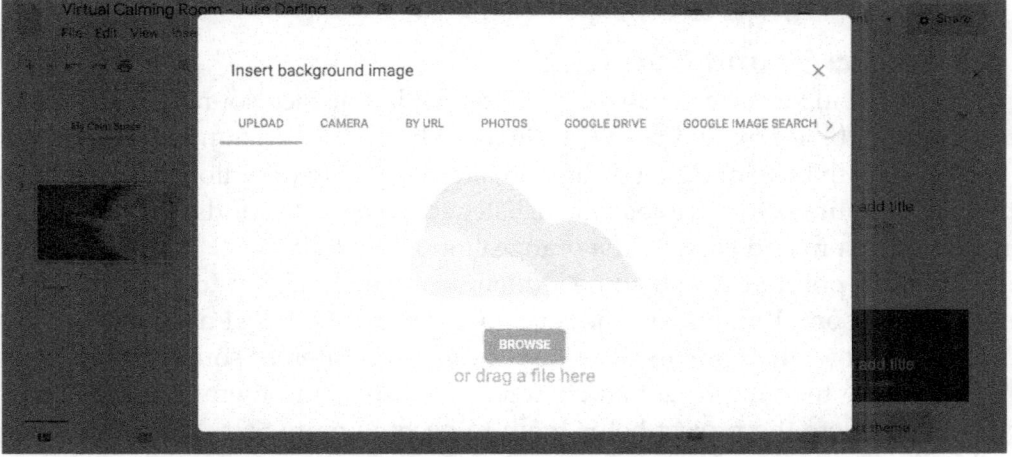

Once they can see that their image has been successfully inserted as the background for their slide, have them click the button that says "Done" in the lower right corner of the pop-up window.

Figure 4.26 Virtual Calming Room

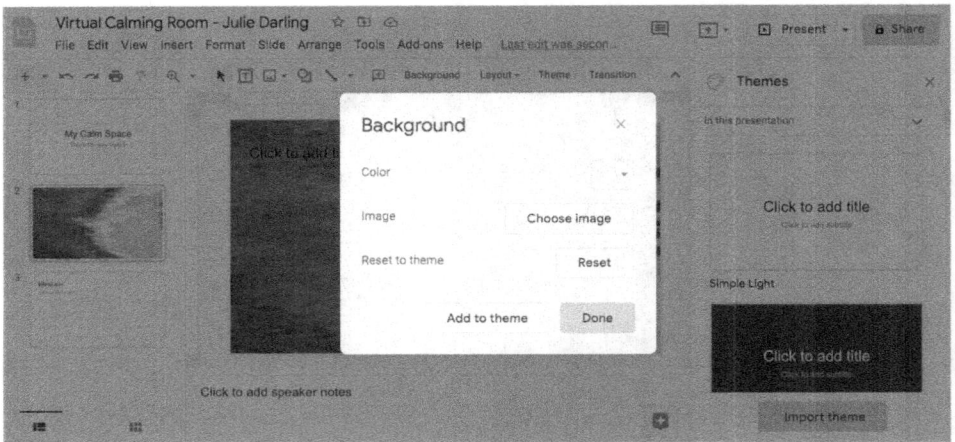

## Step 12: Search for a Sound to Add to Your Calming Room
Now it's time to add sound to the virtual calming rooms! Have your makers search a site with free music. I like Dig CCMixter (http://dig.ccmixter.org/), so will be using that for these instructions. Note that Dig CCMixter is *not* specifically filtered for kids. You may want to explore it yourself before using it with your students. Once kids are on the free music site, have them search by a keyword that is likely to give them calming sounds; some terms they can try include: "ambient," "calm," "instrumental," or "rain."

Figure 4.27 Virtual Calming Room

## Step 13: Find a Sound You Like
Sound file results will have two colorful boxes on the left of each sound. The triangle "play" button in the first, blue box will allow students to listen to the sounds. The orange box to the right of that, with the cloud in it, is the first step to take to download the sound from the cloud to their computer. Once students have listened to several sounds, they should pick one for their calming room and click on the orange cloud next to it.

Note: This is a point at which some students get stuck, trying to pick a perfect sound for their calming room. If they're stuck, remind them that they just need to find one that is good enough for now; they can always swap it out for a different sound later. Cueing them to understand why they might get stuck here and scaffolding them in taking steps to get unstuck and complete the project helps them to become more Self-Aware and encourages Responsible Decision-Making.

## Step 14: Give Credit for Use of the Sound
When students click on the orange box with the cloud next to their sound, a pop-up window will appear. Have them copy credit information first by clicking on the box in the lower left-hand corner that says, "Copy to Clipboard."

Use Multimedia to Share Our Stories    93

Figure 4.28 Virtual Calming Room

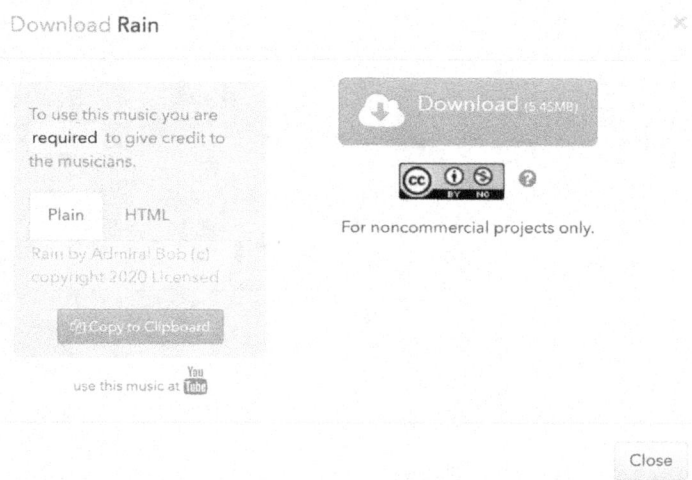

They will get a second pop-up box with instructions on copying the citation information "Control (or Command) + C to copy"; have them use Control + C on a PC or Command + C on a Mac to copy this information. Note: Tell kids to leave this pop-up open; they'll need to navigate back to it to finish downloading their sound.

Figure 4.29 Virtual Calming Room

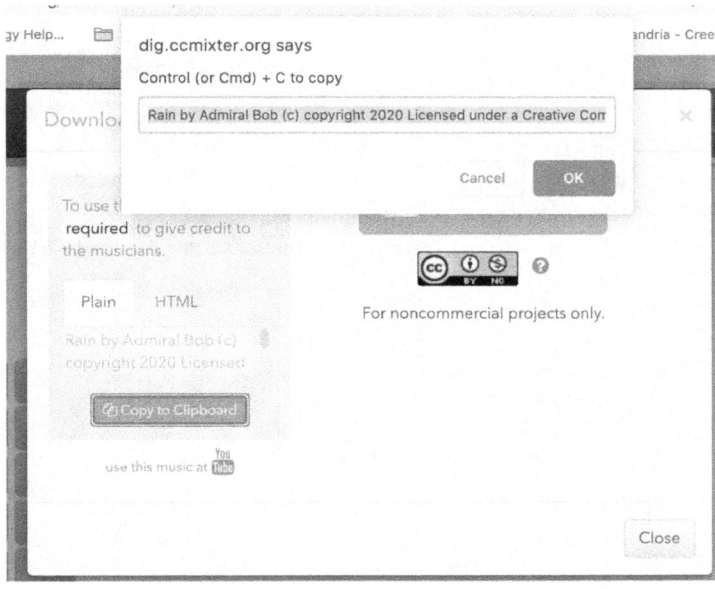

## Step 15: Paste the Sound Citation into the 3rd Slide of the Google Slideshow

Have kids head back to their 3rd slide, the one titled Bibliography, and paste their sound citation information into the slide using the shortcut control + V (PC) or Command + V (Mac).

You'll notice that the citation formatting for the sound file and the image file is different. Depending on the age of the students you're working with, you may want to use this as an

## 94 Use Multimedia to Share Our Stories

opportunity to learn about the correct way to format citations using MLA, APA, or Chicago. However, if you're working with younger students, just teaching them that they *should* give credit may be good enough at this juncture.

Figure 4.30 Virtual Calming Room

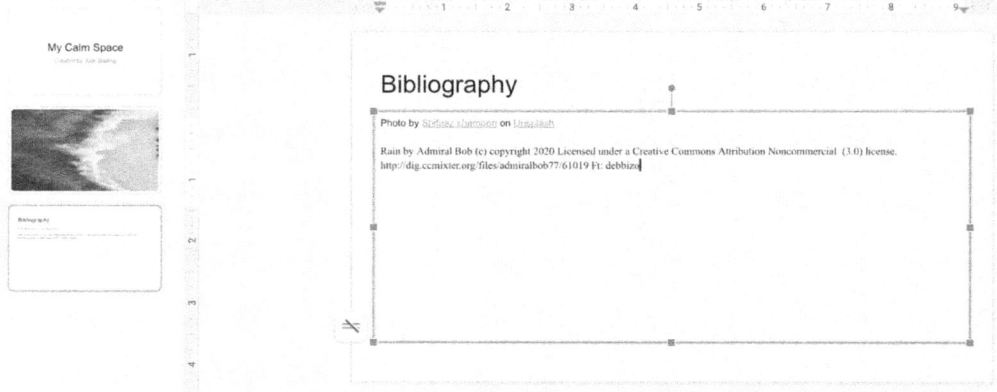

## Step 16: Download the Sound File to Your Computer

Now kids need to finish downloading the sound to their computer. Have them click on the blue download cloud on the top right side of the pop-up.

Figure 4.31 Virtual Calming Room

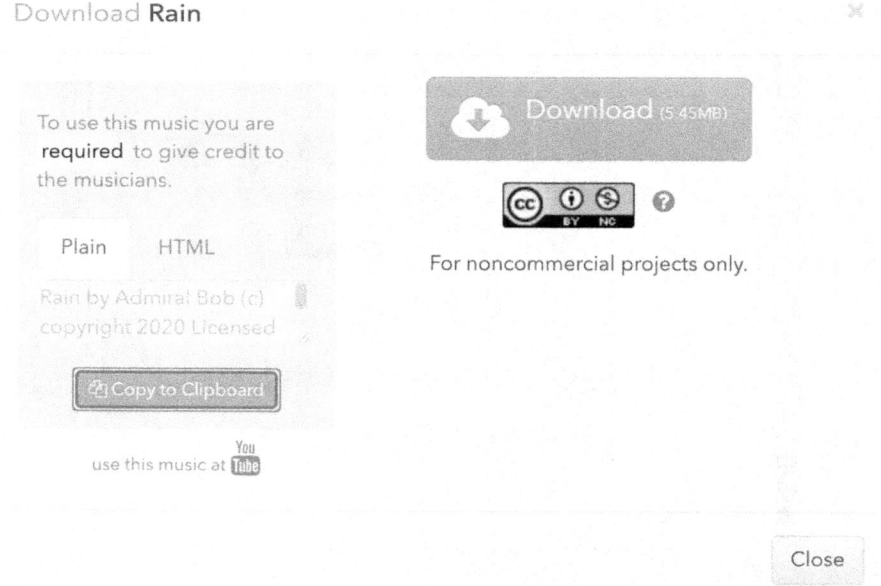

## Step 17: Click the Three Stacked Dots

The song will start playing, but the sound still isn't downloaded; there are two more steps! Tell kids to click the three stacked dots to the right of the song.

A "Download" option will pop up. Have them click on it to download the song to their Downloads folder.

Figure 4.32 Virtual Calming Room

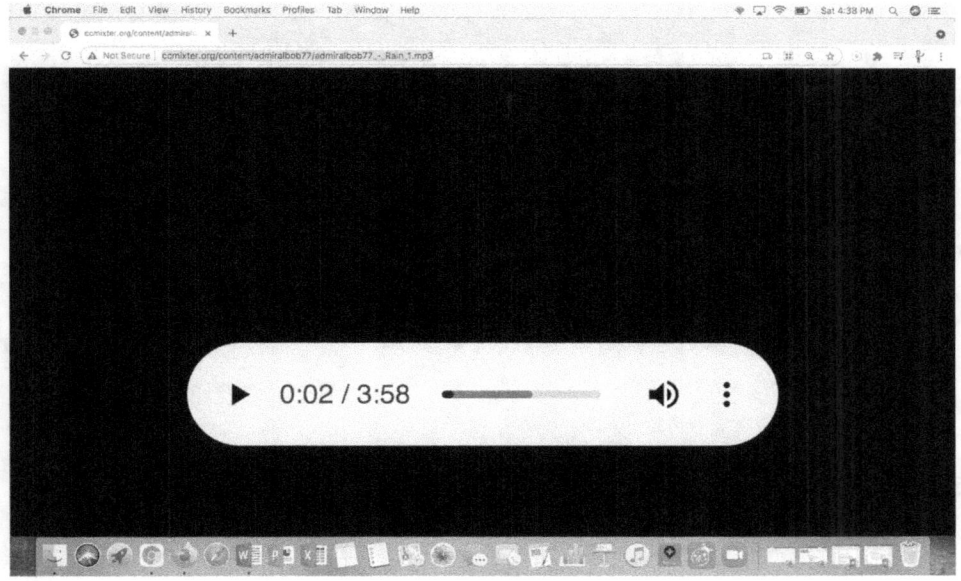

Figure 4.33 Virtual Calming Room

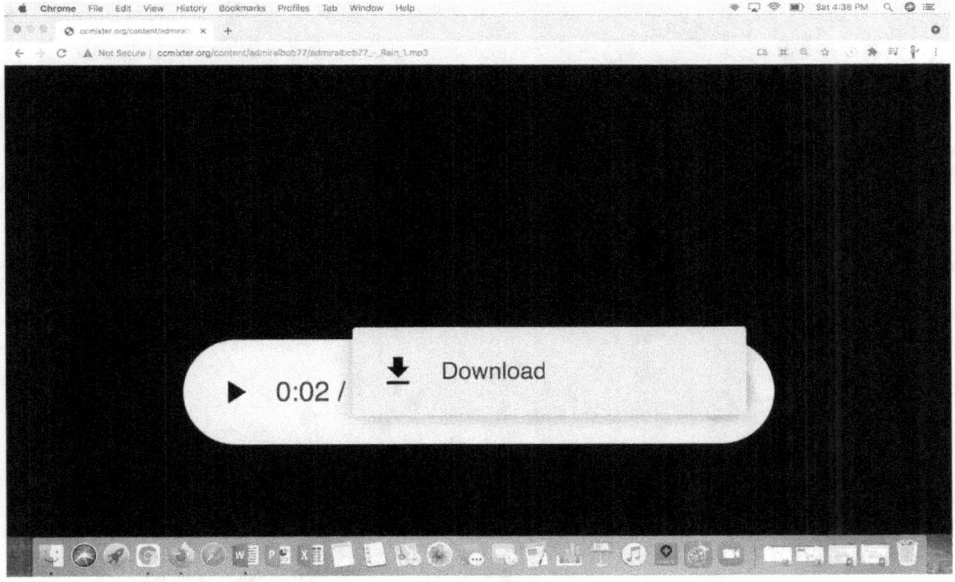

## Step 18: Upload the Sound File to Your Google Drive

Next, students need to upload the sound file to their Google Drive (before they can insert it into their slides). So, have them head back to their Google Drive and select New > File Upload.

Tell them to make sure that they're looking in their Downloads folder for the sound file and have them double-click or click and select once they've located their sound file (it will likely end in the file extension .mp3). They should get a pop-up confirmation in the lower right-hand corner in Google Drive to indicate that their sound file upload was successful.

96   Use Multimedia to Share Our Stories

Figure 4.34 Virtual Calming Room

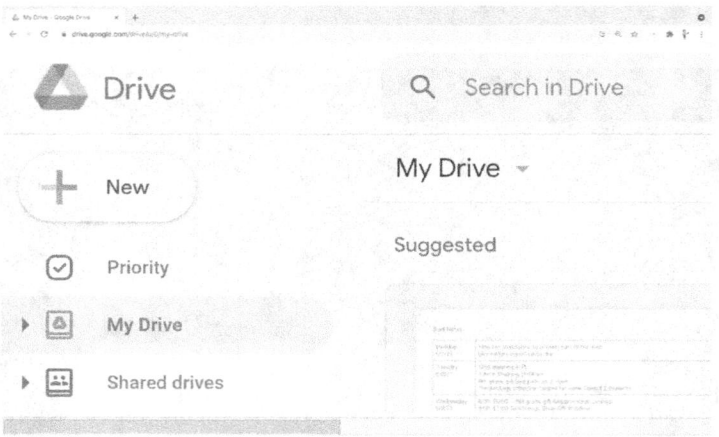

Figure 4.35 Virtual Calming Room

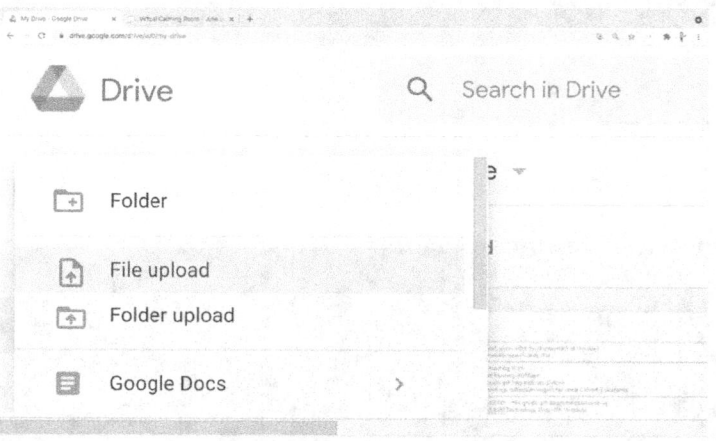

Figure 4.36 Virtual Calming Room

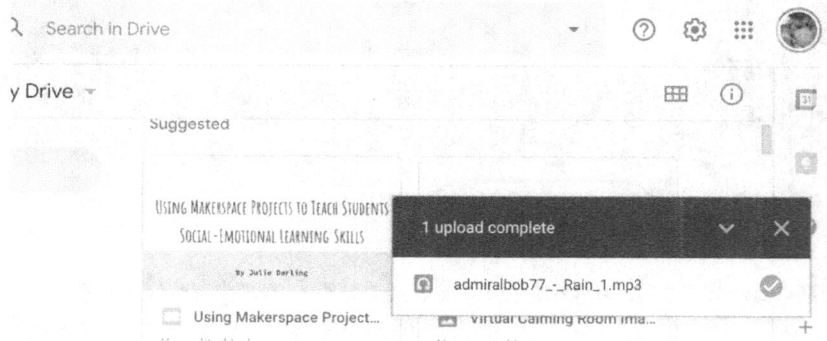

## Step 19: Insert the Sound File into Your Google Slides

Ask kids to head back over to their Virtual Calming Room slides. Have them click on the second slide to select it.

From the top bar (just under their title), have them click Insert > Audio.

Tell kids to make sure that "My Drive" is selected; then double-click, or click on the sound file and click select, to insert the sound into their virtual calming room.

Use Multimedia to Share Our Stories    97

They'll get a pop-up notification that says, "creating audio." They'll see a speaker icon appear on their slide, a bar with the sound time listed, and a play button, and to the far right some audio formatting options. Instruct them to feel free to customize as they see fit (or just leave it as is).

Congratulations! The audio/visual virtual calming room is complete!

**Figure 4.37** Virtual Calming Room

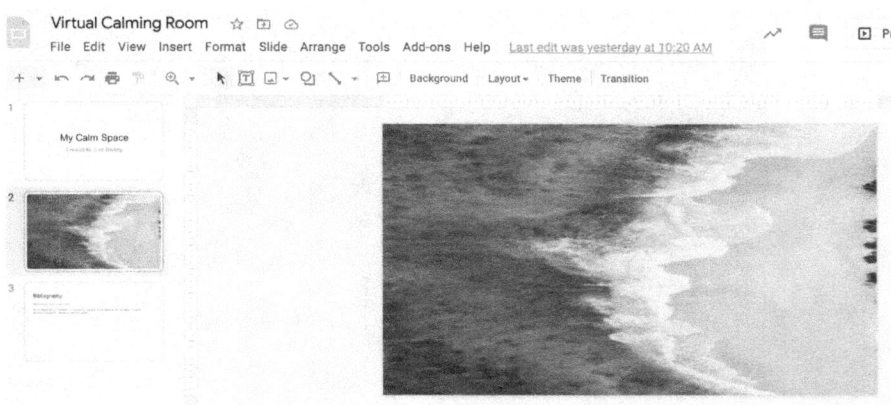

**Figure 4.38** Virtual Calming Room

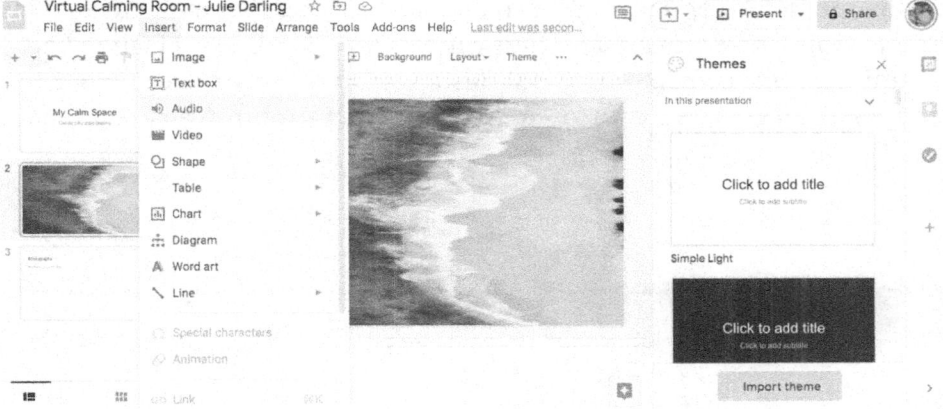

**Figure 4.39** Virtual Calming Room

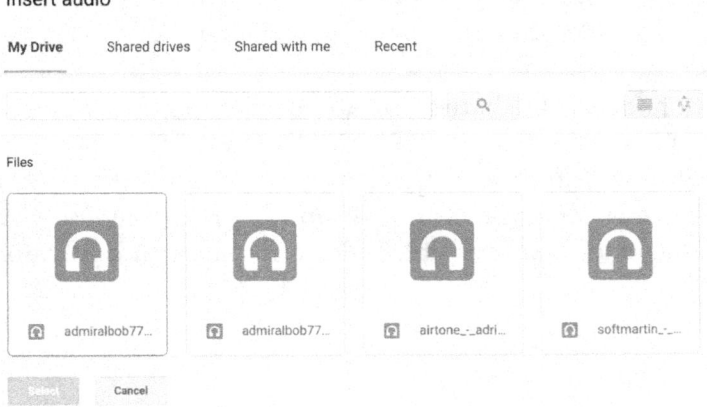

## 98  Use Multimedia to Share Our Stories

Figure 4.40 Virtual Calming Room

### Celebration

Celebrate by sharing the students' virtual calming rooms as a resource that others can use. This helps kids to develop Social-Awareness in two ways: students become aware that everyone is unique in the combination of sounds and images that make them feel calm, and they're also providing a resource that others can utilize when they're feeling bad. You could share the calming rooms by collating the slideshows, linking the slideshows with a site like wakelet.com, or even creating your own virtual calming room website to share with the world.

## Conclusion

Use videos and podcasts in your makerspace to engage kids and give them a voice. Consider your budget, and what equipment you already have. Think about what you might be able to afford, to make video and audio production even better. Consider using a green screen to increase engagement.

Have kids create podcasts to share news about your organization and to discuss topics that they care about. Give your makers a voice, with a much further reach, by allowing them to create videos about topics that are important to them. Teach students to create podcasts, videos and personalized virtual calming rooms to encourage Self-Awareness, Social-Awareness, Self-Management, Responsible Decision-Making and Relationship Skills.

# Chapter 5

# Facilitate Passion Projects

One of the best uses for makerspace is passion projects. Passion projects are powerful. When done right, they become a super-charged combination of two of the most engaging educational strategies: making real-world connections and tapping into student-driven interests. These increase student engagement, exponentially. Woven together, the results are incredible. Allowing students to use makerspace to explore their passion projects gives them additional tools to take these projects even further.

Over the past several years, I've taken thousands of kids through this passion project journey, from idea to final project. Some have continued to pursue their passion projects even beyond my class. One pair of students even completed a book and published it on Amazon! In this chapter, I'll take you from start to finish through how to scaffold passion projects. We'll start with strategies for working with groups with the assumption that you may be managing a full class – solo. However, we'll also cover how to do this for kids working independently. To keep you and your makers from getting stuck, let's start with hurdles, and the scaffolding to navigate around them.

## Activities and Resources Included in This Chapter

- Activity 1: My Favorite Things – Introducing Passion Projects
- Handout: My Favorite Things
- Activity 2: Optional Read-Aloud *What Do You Do with an Idea?*
- Activity 3: Brainstorming
- Handout: Passion Projects Brainstorming Instructions
- Activity 4: Forming Groups, Making a Plan and Getting Feedback
- Handout: Passion Projects Planning and Feedback
- Handout: Passion Project Rubric
- Activity 5: Students Anticipating Obstacles
- Activity 6: Assigning Roles
- Activity 7: A Lesson on Slideshow Design and Presentation Delivery
- Activity 8: Final Presentations
- Independent Passion Projects Overview
- Handout: Independent Project Planning Form
- Facilitating Student Makers as Mentors

DOI: 10.4324/9781003238072-5

## Passion Project Hurdles and Scaffolding When Working in Groups

With passion projects I've encountered some consistent hurdles, the most significant of which is simply getting kids started. Kids are used to teacher-directed projects. For some, being given the choice to pursue something that they're passionate about seems overwhelming. That's why I don't tell them too much about what they're doing – at first. We begin by simply thinking about personal interests. Start with the "My Favorite Things" activity.

## Activity 1: My Favorite Things – Introducing Passion Projects

Estimated Time: 30 minutes.
　　Materials: Copies of the My Favorite Things Handout for all students.
　　Learning objectives:

- Students will list several things that they like.
- Students will identify activities that they enjoy spending time doing.

Social-Emotional Skill:
　　Self-Awareness (CASEL's SEL Framework):

- Students will analyze their personal likes and preferred activities.

## Handout: My Favorite Things

Name: _____ Date: _____

Think about your interests, and the things that you like. Write or draw your answers to the following questions.

What are your favorite:

Color(s)_____

Animal(s)_____

Food(s)_____

Sport(s)_____

Hobby(ies)_____

If you had free time right now, what would you do with it?

## Explain Passion Projects

Next, introduce the idea of passion projects. Ask: What does it mean to be passionate about something? Based on student responses (and any clarification you add) ask what they think a passion project is. Once they've given you some responses that indicate that they're starting to understand the idea, give them more details. Tell them they'll be given a big chunk of time, in class, to explore, investigate, *maybe even build* something they're interested in. Explain that this passion project will be on a topic that they themselves choose.

## Activity 2: Optional Read-Aloud *What Do You Do with an Idea?*

Estimated time: 10 minutes.
    Materials: 1 copy of the book *What Do You Do with an Idea* by Kobi Yamada
Learning objective:

- Students will be able to identify some specific ways that the protagonist in this story was able to persevere, and transfer those ideas to goals for their passion projects.

Social-Emotional Skills:
    Social Awareness (CASEL's SEL Framework):

- Students will think about the story from the protagonist's perspective.

Self-Awareness (CASEL's SEL Framework):

- Students will transfer the message from the story to their own ideas and experiences.

I find that a read-aloud is really helpful here. *What Do You Do with an Idea?* (by Kobi Yamada, illustrated by Mae Besom) is a fantastic book that I like to use as the passion project launch. Before you read it, give them this prompt: "When I'm finished reading this book, I'm going to ask you to tell me why you think I read *this book* to you . . . before starting our passion projects journey." When I finish reading this book, my 6th graders will often clap (the book really is that good).
    Possible takeaways from *What Do You Do With an Idea?*

- Don't give up your idea.
- Give your idea the attention it needs.
- Don't listen to other people if they tell you that your idea isn't good; this is your idea and you understand it better than they do.
- Changing the world for the better is possible; positive changes start with ideas from *you*.

# Activity 3: Brainstorming

Estimated time: 20–30 minutes.
   Materials:

- Sticky notes at each work station
- Writing utensils for all students
- Four pieces of paper on a table at the front of the room, one with each of these labels: "Myself," "My School," "My Community," and "The Whole World"
- Copies of the Passion Projects Brainstorming Instructions Handout at each work station.

Brainstorming activity preparation details:

- Make sure each work station has enough chairs for the maximum number of kids you want to work together in a group.
- Have large piles of colorful sticky notes, or sticky note sized paper (perhaps recycled – at least 20 pieces per kid) at each work station, and something for each kid to write with. Writing utensils can be colorful, and varied, to make it fun.
- At the front of the room, place four pieces of paper with one of these words/ phrases (one per paper): Myself, My School, My Community, and The Whole World. Make sure that these papers are spaced out so that lots of the kids' papers/ sticky notes will fit around each one. This is going to both help give them a focus and tie in social-emotional learning.

Learning objectives:

- Students will develop original ideas for potential passion projects.

Social-Emotional Skills:
   Responsible Decision-Making (CASEL's SEL Framework):

- Students will identify who will benefit from their passion project ideas.

Social Awareness (CASEL's SEL Framework):

- Students will demonstrate active listening skills.
- Students will communicate ideas with others in their group.

Brainstorming should be your next activity to keep kids from getting stuck. Some of the most innovative technology companies start their brainstorming sessions by producing wild, outlandish ideas (before dialing these back). This is a good way to start. It encourages your makers to be innovative, and to do outside-the-box thinking. Brainstorming by following these steps also utilizes Responsible Decision-Making when your makers think about the ways in which their ideas can promote the well-being of others, and Relationship Skills as they communicate and listen to others' ideas.

## Brainstorming Activity Instructions – For You

If you're having your makers work in groups (which I would recommend to make management easier), have kids sit down next to other kids they think they might like to work with. The final work groups will ultimately also depend on whether they can come to a consensus about the topic for their projects, but this is a good starting point. Give them a few general boundaries.

Here are some suggested rules:

1. Nothing involving actual money (it adds a layer of complexity you may not want)
2. The topic has to be school-appropriate (they should ask if they aren't sure)
3. No weapons

Anything else should be fair game at this point.

Give your makers a couple of wild example ideas: maybe you want to build a bicycle that you can ride on the ceiling, or create a whole fashion line of clothing for your cat. Tell them that they will write *one wild idea* per paper/sticky note and see how many they can come up with in 4 minutes. At the end of that 4-minute mark, they'll get a chance to collaborate with the other makers at their tables (this helps them get started with Self-Awareness before branching out to Relationship Skills). Set a timer, and count them off – "on your marks, get set, go!!!"

At the 4-minute mark, get their attention and tell them it's time to collaborate with others at their tables. This collaboration helps them work at Relationship Skills. Help scaffold this by emphasizing that everyone has a voice, and that all voices and ideas should be celebrated. You may need to prompt kids to brainstorm strategies for making sure that everyone has a voice (noting again that there are no bad ideas). Help kids come up with questions they might ask each other during the collaboration brainstorming session.

# Handout: Passion Projects Brainstorming Instructions

1. Sit down at a table with people you think you might like to work with. Make sure you have:
   - Something to write with
   - Sticky notes/papers to write on
2. You will spend 4 minutes brainstorming *by yourself*. Write *one* idea per paper/sticky note. Write as *many* as you can, as *fast* as you can!
3. You have 4 minutes to work with others at your table. Make sure that:
   - Everyone has a chance to talk
   - Everyone is celebrated for their good ideas

Here are some questions you might ask or say to others in your group:

What's your favorite idea so far? I really like that idea, have you thought about maybe . . .? Tell me more about . . . What else could you ask or say?

4. Choose one (or more) of the ideas that *you* wrote down. Think: Is it something that could help:
   - You (for example, it will help you learn something new)
   - Your school
   - Your community (this could be your neighborhood, sports team, church, synagogue, mosque, or any other community that you're part of)
   - The whole world?

*Your* idea is a *good* idea whether it just benefits you, the whole world, or anything in between. This part is just to get you thinking.

5. Once you've chosen your idea(s), one group at a time is going to come place their papers/stickies next to the paper(s) that say, "You," "Your School," "Your Community," or "The Whole World" (who it benefits).
6. Now we are going to do a gallery walk! Half of the groups will read the papers/stickies; the other half will clean up their spaces. Then you'll switch.
7. Once everyone has had a chance to participate in the gallery walk, collect your own papers/stickies and write/stick your favorite ideas to the back of your "My Favorite Things" paper.

### Narrow It Down and Make a Plan

The brainstorming session is energizing and exciting! It's important to keep that momentum going. Don't let too much time pass before giving your makers the opportunity to start drafting a plan. I usually let kids have a full day to think their ideas through. At the end of the brainstorming session, I tell them that during the next class they will form groups, pick an idea, and make a plan.

## Activity 4: Forming Groups, Making a Plan and Getting Feedback

Estimated time: 45–60 minutes.

Materials: A copy of the Passion Projects Planning and Feedback Handout for each group.

Learning objectives:

- Students will work to form a group, make a plan, and give constructive feedback to another group.

Social-Emotional Skills:

Relationship Skills (CASEL's SEL Framework):

- Students will use effective communication to form groups with others with similar interests.
- Students will formulate and share constructive/helpful feedback with other groups.
- Students will work to make certain that all voices in their group are heard.

Social Awareness (CASEL's SEL Framework):

- Students will consider the perspectives of others in their group.

Responsible Decision-Making (CASEL's SEL Framework):

- Students will write out details and steps that will allow those outside of their group to understand the direction and scope of their project.

Self-Awareness (CASEL's SEL Framework):

- Students will work to identify any frustration points they may have when working in groups.

Self-Management (CASEL's SEL Framework):

- Students will identify and pursue a collective goal.
- When frustration points are identified, students will figure out solutions to help themselves navigate these.

Working in groups on passion projects also requires utilizing CASEL's entire SEL Framework. Some students will struggle at this point, and some groups will have trouble reaching a consensus about what they'd like to pursue. You'll want to decide ahead of time how many students you'll allow to work in groups and if they'll be allowed to work independently. My rule is that groups can be as large as they want, but no one is allowed to work by themselves. This ensures that the Social-Emotional skills that come from working in a group are being developed.

Once students have found others with similar interests, it's time to make a plan. You can use the Passion Projects Planning Form on the next page to help scaffold this. This assignment is two-fold because after they've come up with a solid plan groups also need to seek out written peer feedback. It works best if two groups give each other feedback (and they aren't allowed to move on to the next step until they've provided helpful/constructive feedback for each other).

Make sure to scaffold what helpful/constructive feedback sounds like, otherwise students will be tempted to just say, "it looks good!" so that they can move on to the next task (and also not risk hurt feelings). Here are some sentence starters to give your makers:

- What if?
- How will you . . .?
- Have you considered?
- Tell me more about how that will work . . .
- What materials will you need to . . .

## Handout: Passion Projects Planning and Feedback

Names of Group Members:

_____

_____

_____

Describe your passion project in **as much detail as possible**. Include what steps you'll need to take to complete your project. Consider adding drawings and diagrams. Use the back of this paper or staple additional papers to this sheet if you need more space for your plan.

_____

_____

_____

_____

_____

_____

After you've completed your plan, work with another group to provide each other with **helpful/constructive** feedback. Have them write their feedback in the space on the back of this paper.

I emphasize that just because feedback is given, it doesn't mean you have to take it. However, it's also really important to get the perspective of other people. Tell your makers that other people may think of something that you haven't. This can make your plan a lot better. I give examples of times when I was doing something important to me: my proposal for creating a makerspace that I was presenting to our Superintendent; an important email about a hot-button issue; my résumé for a job that I really wanted. I may ask as many as five people – whose opinions I respect – to take a look and give me honest feedback. If they were to just tell me "it looks good," I would assume they hadn't actually read it, or maybe just skimmed it, and I would feel disappointed that they didn't want to help me to make it better. I make sure I ask people who care enough to take the time to take my entire project apart.

Tell kids that they should show their peers that they care about them, and want them to be successful by providing feedback to help make their projects even better. Giving helpful feedback is part of CASEL's SEL Framework "Responsible decision-making: The abilities to make caring and constructive choices about personal behavior and social interactions across diverse situations." Giving someone else constructive feedback, with the aim of helping them to make their project better, is a caring choice.

While students are working on their plans, I hand out the rubric for their final presentations. I explain each of the three categories that I'm using to grade them, and what a top grade in each will look like. I've included my rubric in the next handout; feel free to use or adapt it. Since the projects are varied, it's important to grade using criteria that work with any type of project. This is why I grade on three factors; connect, evolve, and result.

**Connect** addresses the connections that the projects make in helping others (or yourself) and also connecting with the audience during the presentation. Clear communication is part of Relationship Skills (CASEL's SEL Framework). Clear communication is also part of doing well in this part of the rubric. Creating something that helps *others* ties into Social Awareness (CASEL's SEL Framework). Making something that helps *yourself* aids in developing Self-Awareness (CASEL's SEL Framework).

**Evolve** helps to teach your makers that their first draft is not going to be their best one. It highlights the need to keep developing their idea, change strategies when things aren't working and understand that making mistakes is part of what can make your final project even better. This allows them to take risks and helps them to develop a growth mindset. Having a growth mindset is also an aspect of Self-Awareness (CASEL's SEL Framework).

**Result** gives your makers the opportunity to share what they learned through the process of developing their passion project. They can speak to what they learned, and the overall effort they put into the project. This is part of communicating effectively, a facet of Relationship Skills (CASEL's SEL Framework).

# Handout: Passion Project Rubric

|  | Basic Understanding | Progressing toward Expectations | Meeting Expectations | Exceeding Expectations |
|---|---|---|---|---|
| *CONNECT* Through our passion project we are able to make connections . . . | **We can:** **Identify** our passion. **Share** our passion project. | **We can:** Make **a connection** between our passion project and how it benefits us, our school, our community, and/or the world. **Convey** details regarding our passion project to others. | **We can:** Make **specific connections** between our passion project and how it benefits us, our school, our community, and/or the world. **Convey** details regarding our passion project to others in a way that **allows them to understand** our project. | **We can:** Make **deep connections** between our passion project and the way(s) in which it could benefit us, our school, our community, and/or the world. **Convey** our passion project in great detail to others in a way that **allows them to** *clearly* **understand** our project. |
| *EVOLVE* Our passion project has changed and evolved from our initial idea. | **We can:** **Identify a few ways** in which our project has **changed** from the initial idea. | **We can:** **Share several examples** of how our project has **changed** from the initial idea. | **We can:** **Identify ways** in which our project has **improved** from the initial idea. | **We can:** **Identify very specific ways** in which our project has **improved and evolved** from the initial idea and provide **documentation** (artifacts, prototypes, storyboarding, etc.) **regarding how** those changes have occurred. |
| *RESULT* Through our passion project we learned and perhaps created something significant and/or tangible. | **We can:** **Describe** something that we learned and/or show something that we created. | **We can:** **Identify** some specific ways in which we learned through this project and give/show examples. | **We can:** **Demonstrate** what we learned through this project and give/show examples. | **We can:** **Clearly demonstrate** what we learned through this project and give/show examples that indicate **significant effort**. |

## Activity 5: Students Anticipating Obstacles

Estimated time: 10–15 minutes.
Learning objectives:

- Students will analyze their plan and identify potential obstacles.

Social-Emotional Skills:
Responsible Decision-Making (CASEL's SEL Framework):

- Students will work to determine if their project is realistic when considering time, resources, and any other constraints.
- If success is unlikely, students will adapt their plan to draft something that has a better chance at success.

Relationship Skills (CASEL's SEL Framework):

- Students may need to compromise within their group, to create a plan that can be agreed upon.

Now that they have a plan and have received some feedback, ask students to think about what could prevent them from being successful with their passion projects. What obstacles do they anticipate? How could they overcome these obstacles? Explain that when we're pursuing our passions there are always two factors that can impact how far anyone gets: time and resources. Explain how much time they'll have to complete their projects and what resources they have access to; in makerspace, recycled boxes, found objects, at home, online. They'll need scaffolding to determine whether their plan is realistic. They may also need help compromising, figuring out a new plan, and scaling their project down to what can be realistically accomplished. While students work through these questions, make sure you check in with each group to help them think through their plan and the steps they need to take to complete it.

## Activity 6: Assigning Roles

Estimated time: 10 minutes.
Learning objective:

- Students will identify roles relevant to their projects.

Social-Emotional Skills:
Relationship Skills (CASEL's SEL Framework):

- Students will work collaboratively to determine who will assume each role.

Social Awareness (CASEL's SEL Framework):

- Students will recognize each other's strengths and use these to determine which roles they'll be assigned.

Self-Management (CASEL's SEL Framework):

- Students will make safe and responsible choices while using tools and resources.

The time constraint issue can be partly addressed by having the students assign roles and divide tasks. This is a good next step before students start developing their projects. If groups are bigger, multiple students can be assigned to the same role. If students are working in pairs, each student will have to take on multiple roles. Here are some possibilities:

**Leader/Helper:** This role keeps everyone on track, checks in throughout the project, and helps anyone, in any of the other roles, when they need help. The student in this role will have lots of opportunities to work on Social Awareness and Relationship Skills (CASEL's SEL Framework).

**Presentation Maker:** Creates slides, a video, a physical poster, or whatever other components are needed for the final presentation.

**Builder:** Gathers materials, builds the prototype, and makes additional iterations based upon feedback (from inside and outside of the group) and testing. This may not be applicable for all projects.

**Researcher:** Researches using online resources and printed materials. May also seek out expert feedback and set up interviews.

## Activity 7: A Lesson on Slideshow Design and Presentation Delivery

Estimated time: 30–45 minutes.
Learning objectives:

- By the end of the lesson students will understand strategies for creating an effective slideshow.
- Students will understand and be able to demonstrate good presentation delivery techniques.

Social-Emotional Skills:
Self-Awareness (CASEL's SEL Framework):

- Students will identify slide design and presentation delivery strategies that they need to practice or tweak.

Relationship Skills (CASEL's SEL Framework):

- Students will practice together to refine their presentation delivery, and help each other improve.

Responsible Decision-Making (CASEL's SEL Framework):

- Students will develop a backup plan for anticipated issues.

Before the final presentation, I give my kids a mini-lesson on how to design a slideshow and deliver an excellent presentation. I try to model each of these points for them as I explain them. Here's what I cover.

## Slide Design

- Slides can have light text on a dark background or dark text on a light background. Don't put dark text on a dark background or light text on a light background. No one can read that!
- Don't put a lot of words on your slides. The most you should have is two sentences or five bullet points. Less is better.
- A good design for a slide is 1 image and 1 main takeaway point. If you have too many things going on – moving pieces, videos, GIFs – it's hard for your audience to pay attention to what you're trying to tell them.
- When using images, make sure you give credit.

## Presentation Delivery

- Make eye contact, or fake it. You can look at people's foreheads, and sometimes that feels less scary. They can't tell the difference.
- Stand up and take up space; draw your audience's eyes to you.
- Make sure to project your voice. Everyone should be able to hear your words – including those sitting at the back.
- Don't "side" the room. Take time to look at everyone in your audience. Never have your back facing one side of the room for your whole talk.
- Practice and time yourself. Make sure you can finish within the time you're given.
- Watch for fillers such as "um," and uptalk (where it sounds like you're ending every sentence with a question). Practicing more, and slowing down, can help you stop doing these.
- Always have a back-up plan in case of worst-case scenario. For example, take photos or videos of whatever you've built just in case it falls apart or is left at someone's house. Make sure everyone has access to the presentation in case a group member is absent.

# Activity 8: Final Presentations

Estimated time: 10–15 minutes for each presentation.
Learning objectives:

- Students will distill everything learned from their passion projects into an engaging presentation.
- Students will address the topics outlined in the rubric during their presentation.
- Students will utilize best practices for presentations.

114   Facilitate Passion Projects

Social-Emotional Skills:
Relationship Skills (CASEL's SEL Framework):

- Students will work together, and practice their presentation ahead of time.
- Students will work to reframe projects *as a group*, based upon what they learned and how it evolved.

Responsible Decision-Making (CASEL's SEL Framework):

- During practice, students will ensure that they're able to present within the allocated time.
- Students will have a back-up plan for anticipated issues.

Self-Awareness (CASEL's SEL Framework):

- Students will work to develop a growth mindset and comfort with mistakes.
- Students will work to reframe projects *independently*, based upon what they learned and how it evolved.

When students deliver the final presentation, everyone should take part. This might mean that kids are assigned different slides to present, or they may decide on another way to divvy it up. They should be given at least one work session to practice their presentation. They may use index cards, depending upon the age of your makers and their presentation style preferences (figuring this out helps them develop Self-Awareness).

One of the most important lessons from makerspace is developing comfort with mistakes. Some of your makers will have started out with extremely ambitious projects. That's great! However, if the project is too ambitious, it's challenging for them not to feel discouraged. That's why it's important to give them an out. When they're giving their final presentations, if they tried and things didn't work out, there is a lot of value in hearing about how the project evolved (see Passion Project Rubric). This part of the process – discussing what worked, what didn't, and what they learned from it – should have just as much, sometimes *even more*, value than the final version of the project. Make sure you bring this up regularly when you're working with your students to help them learn to have a growth mindset (and also become more Self-Aware).

Presentations should always include lessons learned; information about what was tried, what didn't work, what *did* work, and the journey that the makers took in order to end up where they did. The final presentation can be a theoretical project that is well researched. Kids can act as if the audience is a group of potential investors, and they need to sell their ideas. It can also be a prototype or rough draft. This may be as far as they get based upon how much time they had, and what materials and tools they had access to. They may also be able to present a polished final project. That's great if it works out; however, whether or not they reach that final goal *doesn't matter*. What matters *most* is what they learned through the process.

Working on a passion project with a team develops a whole host of SEL skills. However, it also means that likely your makers will need to compromise at some point on the focus of the project. Use group passion projects to help kids develop SEL skills across the full CASEL's SEL Framework.

To really help kids dig into Self-Awareness and explore their own creative thoughts and goals, make sure you give kids the opportunity to explore passion projects independently, too.

## Independent Passion Projects Overview

Estimated time: Varies.

Independent passion projects will vary in time depending upon what students choose to work on, and how much time you have to give them. In our space, some kids finish their project in 10 minutes before moving on to something else; others spend the entire quarter working on an elaborate and complex project. You'll have to decide what guidelines make sense for your makers in your space.

Materials:

- Enough copies of the Independent Project Planning Form so that you have several for each student
- Makerspace Lanyard Inserts: You'll want to print and cut these out in advance, and then have your makers fill them out and put them into their lanyards, to be worn when they're working in the makerspace (visit https://growingmakerspace.com/resources/ for a free downloadable template)

Social-Emotional Skills:
Self-Awareness (CASEL's SEL Framework):

- Students will identify a personal interest to pursue.

Self-Management (CASEL's SEL Framework):

- Students will make safe and responsible choices while using tools and resources.

Responsible Decision-Making (CASEL's SEL Framework):

- Students will think through their project before starting work on it, and look for any obstacles or help they may need in completing their project.

Independent passion projects, often referred to as "Genius Hour," give your makers the chance to take an idea and run with it. These are wonderful for "developing interests and a sense of purpose," a facet of Self-Awareness according to CASEL's SEL Framework. This is how I teach my elective class with a teaching partner. Managing 31 kids working on 31 independent projects requires at least two people; one person to troubleshoot a tool or a more complex (more time-consuming) issue, and another person to circulate, making sure kids are making safe choices, and also to answer quick questions.

## Getting Students Started

For the most part, it's easy to get makers started on independent projects. In fact, it's often challenging to get them to plan, as they're so excited to get going. In our makerspace, we start by giving students a tour of the space where we describe the tools and some ideas for projects, and then have them sit down and write out a plan (see next page for the one we use, feel free to adapt it for your needs). Once we look over their plans, they can start getting trained on tools or gather materials and get going.

# Handout: Independent Project Planning Form

Name: _____ Date: _____

I want to make:

_____
_____
_____
_____
_____

The materials and tools I need are:

_____
_____
_____
_____
_____

I need to know more about:

_____
_____
_____
_____
_____

I need training on:

_____
_____
_____
_____
_____

I'll know it's finished when:

_____
_____
_____
_____
_____

## Facilitating Student Makers as Mentors

Learning objective:

- ♦ Students will master tool use and mentor other students in the safe and effective use of tools.

Social-Emotional Skills:
Relationship Skills (CASEL's SEL Framework):

- ♦ Students will show leadership in the makerspace, by mentoring others in how to use tools.

Self-Management (CASEL's SEL Framework):

- ♦ Students will make good choices when using makerspace tools and resources.

Self-Awareness (CASEL's SEL Framework):

- ♦ Students will work to develop their own interests in projects, and then help others who're expressing a similar interest.

As the rotation progresses and our makers develop more skills, they become mentors. This means that they can answer the quick questions for each other. In addition to leadership skills, this gives them agency, and buy-in. It also means my teaching partner and myself can get to students more quickly.

We keep track of which skills our makers are ready to teach with stamped lanyards that they wear around their necks. These are marked with the trainings that they've successfully completed.

## Celebrating Our Successes

Students finish projects at different points. Some are able to complete several projects, while others are only able to finish one or two, depending upon the complexity. Either way, we make sure that we celebrate their creations. All physical objects are put on display with an index card describing the project. We attempt to replicate placards in a museum display by asking our makers to include: the title of the work, their name, a description of what materials were used, and an interesting detail. We also have them include the date and their homeroom teacher's name, so if they forget to take their finished work home, it can be delivered to their classrooms.

When time allows, we also have our makers give presentations, sharing their successes.

## Conclusion

I strongly encourage you to utilize your makerspace for passion projects. Doing so, especially when students work in groups, ties into CASEL's *entire* Core Competencies SEL Framework. I would also encourage you to allow some time for independent passion projects aka Genius Hour. This will give your makers a chance to deeply explore Self-Awareness by "developing interests and a sense of purpose" (CASEL's SEL Framework). Regardless of how you manage them, passion projects are arguably the most powerful use of makerspace tools and materials.

## Chapter 6

# Fund and Supply Your Makerspace

In this chapter we'll take a broad sweep at different ways to fund and supply your makerspace. Having excellent tools and resources will allow you to use your space to empower your makers. Great tools and resources are not always free, and some can be pretty expensive. The suggestions in this chapter will help you get what you need.

Included are ideas for upcycling, bartering or borrowing materials, raising money through fundraisers, and grant writing advice from two experts. Let's start with strategies for getting materials for free.

## Resource Included in This Chapter

- Reproducible: Makerspace Donations Policy

# Getting Stuff for Free (or Close to It)

Before seeking out funding, first look for ways to obtain materials for free. There's no need to raise and spend money on things already available to you at a low cost, or no cost at all. Channels of cheap or free materials are more viable than you might think. Collecting recycled and donated materials, perusing thrift stores, working with local organizations, and utilizing free digital resources can go a long way to supplying your makerspace.

## Recycling and Upcycling

The easiest and cheapest ways to obtain consumable materials is recycling and *upcycling*, or reusing discarded materials to create something better. Once people in your community are aware that you're willing to take their broken items – assuming you are – donations will probably start pouring in. Taking donations can be both a blessing and a curse. Make sure you have a policy in place to communicate to donors what kinds of items are useful for your space. If your policy is too broad, you may find yourself spending a lot of time managing unneeded materials. On the following page is a sample donated materials policy that you are welcome to use or adapt for your own purposes.

DOI: 10.4324/9781003238072-6

## Reproducible: Makerspace Donations Policy

Thank you so much for your donation to our makerspace! We appreciate your generosity; gifts and donations to our makerspace help us to make it more interesting, exciting, and innovative.

### Monetary Donations

Monetary donations to the makerspace will be put toward purchases made at the discretion of our makerspace coordinator. This could mean it is used to purchase a tool or piece of equipment, or it may be used to purchase consumable materials for an upcoming project. If you wish, we can provide you with information about how your money was used as well as give you a receipt for tax purposes. Please just ask.

### Donation of Tools and Materials

Tools and materials will be used or repurposed at the discretion of the makerspace coordinator. Once a tool or consumable material is given over, it is considered makerspace property to be used, repurposed, or recycled as suits our current makerspace needs.

### Materials Frequently Needed

The following items are in high demand in our space:

- Duct tape
- Pillow fill
- Hot glue gun, glue sticks
- LED lights
- Coin batteries
- Copper (conductive) tape

Items that our makerspace is *not* currently accepting include:

- Styrofoam
- Empty plastic food containers
- Cardboard boxes covered with labels
- Large cardboard boxes such as those used to transport a television or piece of furniture

Although I don't advertise it (I don't want to get inundated), I almost always accept outdated or broken tech equipment. Older students can pilfer parts from old equipment to create circuits like simple motors. Younger makers can take things apart with tiny screwdrivers to develop fine motor skills. I save some items that have glass or ink in them – like fax machines or printers – for my most responsible students, coupled with plenty of safety reminders. Other equipment – like old computers, calculators, and toys – I dole out to students who are particularly interested in deconstruction or where it's relevant to their specific projects.

Recycling bins are also a great place to raid for materials. Whenever I bring recycled materials back to my makerspace, it only takes about five minutes for someone to spot it and say, "Oh that's perfect for . . ."

You can also look for free materials out in nature. Take a nature walk with your makers and let them find items like leaves, flowers, rocks, and sticks. Not only does this help get energy out, but it also provides you with free materials for papermaking, Kindness Rocks, or maybe even a bug for a Jurassic Park mosquito-in-amber replica. You never know what amazing projects nature can inspire kids to create!

## Thrift Stores and Garage Sales

Thrift stores are a great place to get cheap consumable materials, especially if you're interested in working with textiles. With the same small amount of cash, you can get a whole lot more fabric at a thrift store than what you would get from fabric and craft stores. You might also find items you can take apart and repurpose. I've asked thrift store managers for (and been given for free) items they were planning on throwing out, such as equipment that was beyond repair.

Garage, yard, and estate sales are also great places to go to get inexpensive materials. I like going to big neighborhood sales where I'm likely to find treasure troves of yarn, felt, beads, and other materials from discarded hobbies. People are also often willing to haggle, if you're into that. If you want your pick of materials, go at the start of sales. If you want items for cheap or even for free, head there at the end.

Regardless of what you buy or take, just make sure to wash everything before putting it into your makerspace.

## Donations from Organizations

Although recycling bins, nature walks, and thrift stores are fantastic for obtaining general items, if you're looking for something specific, you may want to seek out donations from organizations. These organizations might include local crafting, hardware, or big box stores that carry supplies that are useful for making. Most of these organizations can take a tax write-off for donated items or gift cards to be used in their stores, so they have the incentive to provide you with items you might need.

When you approach an organization, you will likely need to speak to the owner or someone in management. You should also be really clear and specific about what you're asking for, and how you'll use the item to benefit the kids in your makerspace.

If you do receive a donation, follow up with them once you receive or use it. I like to include a "feel good" component to the donation acknowledgement. I might have the students write a personalized thank-you note, and I usually take a photo of the students using the donated item. A good rule of thumb is to send the acknowledgement off within a month of receiving the items, or even sooner if possible.

## Free Digital Resources

In addition to acquiring physical materials for your makerspace, you should build up your pool of digital resources. Fortunately, plenty of useful digital resources are available for free. There are many materials available in the public domain – photographs, music, writing, and more – that are copyright free and available for anyone to use. In addition, you can locate resources that use Creative Commons Licensing, or software that is Open Source or free for educational use. Seek these out before paying for digital resources.

## Creative Commons Licensing

Creative Commons has revolutionized the way people use and share digital content. With *Creative Commons Licensing*, anyone can share their work and apply a Creative Commons license to it without needing to pay or consult with anyone to make it official. You can simply download the license you want to use, or copy and paste the source code, and add it to your website.

Conversely, if you'd like to use something that someone else has created, if it has a Creative Commons license, you're free to use it as long as you follow the restrictions given.

## Open Source

*Open source* refers to software that's available for anyone to download, copy, or adapt to suit their needs. The underlying philosophy of open source is that technology – like software and the Internet – should be free. Having more eyes on something as complex as a piece of software also means that more people are testing it, troubleshooting it, and making it better. Rather than paying for expensive software, seek out other such open source (and other free) options when considering resources for your makerspace.

## Free for Educational Use

If you find an expensive piece of software that would work well for your makerspace, it's also worth exploring whether or not there's a version of it that's free (or at least less expensive) for educational use. Usually, companies have a link to download their "for educational use" software directly on their website, along with information on how to download it. If they don't, it may be worthwhile to just contact them and ask. I was able to obtain 30 free licenses for Unity, the extremely powerful, 3D game design software, simply by emailing them and filling out a short form. It's always worth it to ask.

# Bartering or Borrowing

Once you've tried to obtain materials for free (or for dirt cheap), you can also try bartering or borrowing to get the materials and tools you want for your makerspace.

## Barter System

One unique aspect of our makerspace is our use of the *barter system*; when students use consumable materials, we expect them to put something back into the makerspace in exchange.

It might seem better to have the makers just bring in the consumable materials they need for their projects, or perhaps even to have a small selection of materials available for purchase on site. This seems to work well for professional spaces, but kids usually aren't focused enough to know what materials they need in advance and they may not have the money to purchase them. You could tell them what to create and give their grownups a list of specific items, but telling kids what to make is counter to the creative spirit of a makerspace. In addition, it's difficult for kids to explore ideas if they can't freely peruse a stockpile of available materials.

This is where our barter system comes in. Since trades don't have to be exactly equal, kids are free to bring in whatever they want, and your stockpile of materials stays full. For example, if they use duct tape, they can bring in beads. If they print a 3D object, they might bring in some cloth fabric. Whatever they've got at home in a junk drawer suffices. Something off of our makerspace wish list is especially great, but if they just find something interesting in a recycling bin, that works too.

Having your makers bring in numerous, varied materials makes organizing your makerspace more time-consuming. It helps to have a lot of differently shaped bins, boxes, plastic bags, and a good label maker.

The barter system makes the act of labeling and finding good storage containers a continuous process. You should go through and reorganize, label, recycle, and straighten everything at the end of each quarter (or program session). It takes time, but the next group can then find what they need to create.

The barter system keeps things interesting in other ways, too. There's no predicting what students will bring in. Some of it is useful and some of it is a little confusing. I occasionally find myself saying things like, "One paperclip?" or "Huh. Well, that's a good start . . ." or even "um . . . that looks really interesting; can you tell me more about what it's used for? *[What the heck is that?!]*"

## Borrowing Resources from Other Places

You can also obtain tools by borrowing them. If you're interested in a tool or piece of equipment that you want to try out before committing to a purchase, or if it's something only one kid is using for a specific project, this can be your best option. For example, you can collaborate with another makerspace and rotate tools between your spaces.

Some public libraries also have items for checkout. My local public library checks out unusual items like projectors, thermal cameras, die cutters, portable document scanners, microscopes, metal detectors, Arduino starter kits, telescopes, and sewing machines. This is a trend for public libraries around the country.

Additional places you can ask to borrow tools or machines might be local businesses, colleges or universities, or maybe even your colleagues. For example, the tool that the maintenance department uses to cut locks off lockers also works very well for cutting the end off of a toothbrush when making bristlebots.

## Raising Money through Fundraising

Perhaps you can acquire everything you need for free, for dirt cheap, or through bartering or borrowing systems. But if, after trying those strategies, you find yourself needing to buy additional expensive pieces of equipment or more specific materials, you'll need to know how to raise money. This can be done by selling projects, hosting book fairs, official fundraising events, grant writing, or crowdfunding.

### Selling What You Make

Fundraisers certainly aren't new. School bake sales happen so often that they've become a stereotype for fundraising. If you love running bake sales, go for it, but cupcakes and cookies aren't the only items you can sell to raise money for your makerspace. Think about how most public libraries sell used books to fundraise; libraries sell used books because they're so easy to come by, between donations and books removed from their collections. In the same vein, if you want to earn money for a makerspace, the best items to sell are the items you make.

This can play out in a few different ways. For example, if your makerspace is in a school, you might have a makerspace entrepreneurial elective class, where students create items that other people in your school or community want to buy. Students can work in teams or individually to design something, create prototypes, and then take the object all the way through marketing and production. Students can then actually sell the product at the end of the course, as a fundraiser for your makerspace. This can also be a great way to develop partnerships with local businesses. Students can consult with businesses to learn about how production is done on a larger scale and learn about what they can adopt for their own projects. For some of these students, these partnerships may even lead to a career someday.

Instead of an elective class, you can also do something much simpler. For example, you can have a rule that whenever a student 3D-prints an object, or makes a button, or sews a stuffed animal, they make two – one to keep, and one to sell at the makerspace store. However you design it, making items to sell is a logical way to raise funds for a makerspace.

## Book Fairs

If you work in, or your kids attend, a school in the United States, you've likely heard of Scholastic Book Fairs. Scholastic is a company that publishes and sells books that are marketed to kids. The Scholastic Book Fair is one service that they provide where they send cases of books to schools, with materials and supplies to use to display and sell them.

These schools then sell the books to their community and are able to keep some of the profits at the end of the book fair.

For some school librarians, the Scholastic Book Fair provides the only funding that they receive for the entire school year. I'm lucky enough to work in a district that gives me a modest budget for books and processing materials for the library, so my principal allows me to take profits from book fairs like Scholastic's to pay for some of my makerspace's consumable materials.

When you take the profits from the Scholastic Book Fair, you're often allowed to divide them between actual money and Scholastic dollars, which you can use to purchase books and materials from the Scholastic catalogue. The amount that you get is larger if you take all Scholastic dollars, smaller if you take actual money, and somewhere in between if you take some of each, which is what I tend to do. Keep in mind that Scholastic dollars buy more than just books on their site; their online catalogue has featured some maker products in the past, including Makey Makey kits (an "invention" kit that teaches kids about circuits), LittleBits kits (another circuit making kit that uses magnetic pieces), and video cameras.

If you're considering hosting a Scholastic Book fair, you'll need to figure out some logistical matters:

- Who's in charge of making certain that the cash, check, and credit card sales match up with the actual money in the cash register?
- Who's staffing the book fair?
- When is the fair open?
- How do you plan to market the fair?
- Where is it physically located?

Scholastic has people on staff that help you with all of this, but you also need volunteers to make the fair run smoothly. In schools, homeroom teachers usually sign up for a preview time, when kids come through and write down books they're interested in, and a purchasing time, when kids can buy those books or order them, to be delivered later. Having 20 classes come through for two separate 10–15-minute time slots to preview and purchase can be extremely disruptive, as you might imagine. You need a lot of volunteers to help younger kids find the books they want to purchase and determine if they were given enough money to afford them.

Sales from the Scholastic Book Fairs vary depending upon the year and season. In my experience, the biggest profits tend to occur directly before winter break (holiday gift purchases), and especially on evenings when something else like a music performance or project fair is also happening at the school, which creates more foot traffic with parents coming in with their kids.

The profits from these fairs could be over $1,000, but I can't remember ever breaking $2,000 for a single book fair. Perhaps I could have, if I had taken all Scholastic dollars and no actual cash. Your profits could also be in the hundreds, if you don't have a lot of sales or you just have a smaller student population. Scholastic can be tricky with their fairs; if you have great sales, you get a better and bigger fair for the following year, which likely means better profits. The flip side is that if you don't have good sales, your offerings for the following year are smaller, and consequently so are your profits.

You should decide if it's worth it, and whether or not this is something that could work well with your community. Scholastic also isn't the only organization that does this; it just seems to be the most popular. For example, often local independent book stores will partner with you for a book fair, too.

## Makerspace Fundraising Event

You can also raise money for your makerspace with big one-off events. One example of this is a family build night, where you invite families in to explore and try out equipment in the makerspace. An easy way to manage this is to have kid-experts from your makerspace staff various stations and guide families through different activities, as you circle around and help where you're needed. You can prominently place a donation jar where visitors walk in, with a sign for suggested donations, and information about how you'll use the money raised by the event.

You can also try hosting an *official* school (if you're in a school) or mini Maker Faire (if you're in a public library or other makerspace nonprofit organization), where you would work directly with Make Community (the sponsors of Maker Faires across the globe). This could be a great opportunity, *but* there are more rules to abide by. There are guides available online on the Make Community site to walk you through how it works, step by step. You should start planning it at least a year in advance. Register the event with Make Community and they should provide you with checklists, worksheets, and additional information that you need to adhere to, as well as information to help you figure out how to make it successful.

## Crowdfunding

One method of fundraising that has gained popularity with educators in recent years is *crowdfunding*, the act of fundraising by gathering small amounts of money from many different people, usually through an online site. I've had colleagues who successfully raised funds this way for books, 3D printers, and flexible seating options for their classrooms.

There are many sites that can help you crowdfund for your makerspace; Gofundme and Kickstarter are two of the better-known sites, but there are plenty of others. Doublethedonation specializes in matching gifts and Ed.co and DonorsChoose are both aimed at K-12 schools. You might consider having kids involved in producing a marketing video for the campaign.

If you do decide to go this route, it's a good rule of thumb to ask for one item per campaign and run these one at a time, with each campaign lasting a month or two at most in duration. It would probably work well to run a campaign once per quarter, semester, or year.

You can give your current students a list of expensive items that you want for the makerspace and let them vote on which one they're most excited by.

Parents are more likely to fund items that will directly benefit their own kids, so a quick turnaround between obtaining the item and utilizing it in the makerspace is a good way to go, when at all possible. Make sure to send thank-you notes (some sites will automatically do this for you) and take photos of the kids using the item.

# Grant Writing

My makerspace was launched, in large part, upon successfully written grants. Grants are money given by an organization, to be used for a specific purpose. I wrote to several organizations that were seeking grantees from educational organizations for tools and materials for our makerspace. Through successful grant writing, I was able to obtain several years' worth of filament for our 3D printer, an Oculus Rift (virtual reality headset), several 3Doodler (3D drawing) pens, a Makey Makey kit, a SparkFun Inventor's Kit (a kit used to teach electronics and programming with Arduino), several LittleBits STEAM kits (full sets of magnetic "bits" that can be put together to build a multitude of different circuits), and most recently my partner teacher won a grant that paid for the materials for our LEGO door. Grants are wonderful for obtaining specific items that there wouldn't otherwise be funding for, although they can also be used to pay for much more. Some nonprofit organizations are funded entirely through grants.

I've had the most success with grants through local organizations—professional organizations, district educational foundations, and local foundations that focus on educational initiatives. I've had less success with grants given by the State of Michigan and big national grants open to anyone in the country working in education. This is partly due to the sheer competition for these grants, but also because they often target underprivileged schools and the school where I work doesn't qualify.

Although I've had success with grant writing, I'm by no means a professional grant writer. If you're planning on funding your makerspace using grants, someone should spend a chunk of their time devoted to this task, whether yourself or someone else. You may even want to consult a professional grant writer. I had the good fortune of speaking with Laura Russello, a New York City–based Development Consultant, and attending a talk on grant writing for nonprofits given by University of Michigan, Foundation and Grants Librarian, Paul Barrow. This is what I learned.

## Where to Look for Grants

Russello starts looking for grants by searching online subscription databases for foundation and corporate funding. She uses two main databases: Foundation Directory Online and Grant Watch. Once she locates a few possible matches through either one, she visits the Foundation websites to discover more detailed information about what they're interested in funding. This way she can make sure that their focus matches up well with the mission, vision statement, and the specifics of the project that she's seeking funding for.

Barrow also recommends Foundation Directory Online. Additionally, he uses Grantspace.org, which he says has all kinds of information about private sector funding and includes trainings, either free or for a small cost, that cover a plethora of topics, including how to write cover letters, proposals, letters of inquiry, and more.

## Writing Grants

When writing grants, be very specific about how you plan on using the grant and how much everything costs (including tax and shipping). You need to follow through on everything that you write into your grant application, so make sure that you're being realistic with the ways in which you intend to use the funding and what you plan to purchase with it. If you can't follow through, you can try communicating with the granter to see if they're open to the funds being spent in a different way, but be prepared to return the funding if you can't reach an agreement.

The same is true if you spend more or less than anticipated. I asked Barrow what to do if the price of items in your grant changes between when you wrote the grant and when it's accepted; he urged that you always want to ask permission. This is true both in cases when you're hoping for additional funding, like when the price or quantity of needed items increases, as well as when the price of granted items has decreased and you'd like to spend the leftover funding in a related way.

It's also smart to have a backup plan. I have an internal account that has a small amount of funding that I can use if, for example, the cost of an item went up slightly in between requesting the grant and purchasing the item, or to cover costs like shipping.

## Catering Your Proposal to the Grant Organization

According to Russello, every Foundation has its own personality and ideas about what it wants to see, and how it wants you to present the grant information. She advises that if a Foundation puts their contact information online, you should call and request a meeting with the program officer (or other key staff member) to pitch your idea and get their thoughts on how you should proceed. Barrow agrees that reaching out is really important and adds that the norm in the funding world is still to talk to someone on the phone as opposed to just sending an email. If you establish a positive relationship before you submit, hopefully they'll go to bat for you. Either way, their feedback should be very helpful in crafting your proposal.

Russello also says to make sure you thoroughly answer all of the questions that they pose. Some foundations give general operating funds, while some only give grants for projects – frame your proposal to adhere to what these foundations are willing to fund. Be very clear on how you plan on allotting the dollars.

Barrow says that you should look at a foundation's history of giving (which you can look up through Foundation Directory Online) and search for how much they've historically given and what kind of projects they've funded. This makes it easier to figure out whether or not they're likely to fund your project. He also recommends looking at the amounts that an organization has historically granted. If they've never granted more than $5,000 to any one project, you may not want to ask for $10,000. Instead, you might want to ask for $5,000 from them and $5,000 from another source.

If you're seeking government grants, it can get a little trickier, according to Russello. First, you need to figure out if you're looking for local, state, or national government money. You need to determine which government departments issue requests for proposals for makerspace-related funding. Sometimes it's helpful to make a call or visit to an office to discuss local government grants. You can also sign up for listservs through some of the government websites to receive notifications when new proposals are released.

## Following Up with the Grant Organization

Russello recommends that once you submit a proposal, if you haven't heard back in three months or so, give them a call or shoot them an email and ask about when a decision will be made. Follow up until you get a concrete answer. If you do get rejected, ask if they're open to giving feedback. Ask why it was rejected or what you can do next time to make it more appealing. Russello knows of proposals denied for 5 years and granted on the 6th, likely because there was something else that the foundation wanted to do, and because oftentimes foundations change their giving priorities from year to year. Her advice is to persevere. If you get rejected, next time submit for something else or frame it differently; don't submit the same proposal verbatim.

You also need to send an acknowledgement for any grants you receive. Most likely, when you apply for a grant, the application will include information about what's expected in terms of follow-up. However, if this isn't included, make sure to at least send a thank-you note with information about and photographs of how the grant was used.

Grants are a great way to acquire funding, but they're not the only option available to you. If you're building your makerspace while working with a school or library, it may be possible to acquire funds through your organization.

# Public Schools

Public schools in the United States are funded through a combination of federal, state, and local funding; it may be possible to allocate some of these funds towards your makerspace. This is because each source of funding provides money that's earmarked for very specific purposes, purposes that makerspaces might be able to satisfy.

For example, suppose a school millage includes money to be used for technology in the schools. Makerspace equipment would certainly qualify as technology, and if your Principal, Superintendent, or your school board is in your corner, it may be a way to purchase large pieces of equipment like laser engravers, CNC routers, or 3D printers. This is especially true if you can provide evidence that this equipment could be used to benefit the whole district, and maybe even the whole community. Additionally, if you can tie the use of this equipment to curricular standards and the mission statement of your organization, you can build a much stronger case for purchasing them.

Before seeking approval, figure out what equipment you need, how it benefits your school district or community, who will staff the makerspace and if this would be an additional cost, what kind of funding you need for consumable materials and safety equipment, and any other considerations that may be specific to your makerspace. These are the big leagues. Take your time with this. Do your research. Make sure your numbers and rationale are solid.

## Conclusion

Funding your makerspace will be an ongoing challenge that you can tackle in a number of ways. If you're creating a makerspace within an already established organization such as a school or library, and you're keeping it fairly low-key, you might only need to use free or cheap methods like recycling, upcycling, finding materials out in nature, or bartering and borrowing. Make sure you aren't overlooking digital resources within the public domain and that you're seeking out Creative Commons licensing, open source, and free for educational use materials.

If you're looking for a few less expensive materials and tools, hitting thrift stores and garage sales might work. For more expensive or specific items, seek out donations from local businesses, crowdfund, or write grants to get what you need. Don't forget to write thank-you notes! If you aren't already a nonprofit organization, consider forming one; this will give you more options in terms of grants, as well as other advantages.

For general funds, you can host a Scholastic book fair or family build night, or partner with maker media for an official school or mini Maker Faire. You may even be able to procure funding directly through your organization by submitting a proposal to your governing body. Regardless, you'll likely find yourself using some combination of these methods for raising funds and procuring tools and supplies for your makerspace.

# Chapter 7

# Management, Trainings, and Volunteers

Managing a makerspace is no small undertaking, especially if your makers are mostly kids. The challenge is two-fold: you need to keep kids safe, and you can't be an expert at everything. I built, designed, and currently coordinate our makerspace, but I couldn't manage it without my talented partner teachers. In addition, our makerspace wouldn't be as amazing without the help I get from expert volunteers. In this chapter, we'll discuss some of the management and organizational techniques we employ, as well as suggestions for recruiting and managing volunteers.

## Resource Included in This Chapter

- Makerspace Student Safety Contract Handout

## Volunteers

Volunteers are a critical part of my makerspace. Without volunteers, the makerspace wouldn't be nearly as fun, exciting, or interesting. Our volunteers bring outside knowledge and expertise about subjects that they're passionate about. For example, one of my regular volunteers "Gran" is the grandmother of two of my wonderful students, and she's a textiles maven. She comes in once a week for our elective classes, and brings along her knitting machine. With her machine, she helps students create scarves in 20 minutes flat. She also works with students on sewing embroidered pillowcases, quilt panels, and individual student-choice sewing projects. In addition, she stocks our makerspace with yarn, fabric, and thread from her own collection.

Gran is worth her weight in gold, and I wish I could pay her commensurately. Sadly, I don't have funding for paying visiting experts. What I do have is endless gratitude, chocolate in my office, and holiday and end-of-year gifts that I purchase (or make) for my volunteers. This is the best that I can do, and thankfully, it seems to be enough.

DOI: 10.4324/9781003238072-7

When I worked as a public librarian I had a modest budget earmarked for outsourcing expertise on various topics. Having some funding makes getting outside help much easier, but there are other options. Your budget, community, staffing, and the rules that govern your space are going to determine what kind of help you will be able to procure. Your community is going to be the strongest factor in determining what kind of volunteer help you might get. Some places you might look for help could be:

**Senior community centers** – senior citizens often have amazing heritage skills (sewing, woodworking, etc.) that they might be willing to share and they likely have time to share them.

**Parent groups** – parents in groups such as parent teacher associations (PTAs) are usually seeking opportunities to volunteer in ways that benefit their kids.

**Universities** – you may be able to create a partnership with nearby colleges or universities to seek out help from college students, or maybe even professors.

**Businesses** – often large businesses and corporations encourage or even require their employees to volunteer in their communities.

Before accepting volunteers from any of these organizations, you should administer some sort of interview process and a mandatory background check. Some levels of background checks you might consider are:

- At very least a sex offender status search. In the United States, this can be done through the U.S. Department of Justice site: https://www.nsopw.gov.
- A criminal background check. You can hire a company to run this for you.
- Reference checks.

In addition, never leave volunteers alone with students, even those you trust completely. Volunteers are there to contribute knowledge to your makerspace; they're not there to instruct students in your absence. This is primarily for the safety of the kids, but it's also to help facilitate instruction. Experts can teach your makers incredible things, but they may have absolutely no idea about how to manage a group of kids. You should want to help with this, and diplomatically step in when needed.

If you do want your volunteers to teach (and not just present), consider pairing them up. Requiring volunteers to work in groups of two or more is also a good safety measure. At the end of a semester, or after a one-off presentation, make sure to send some sort of thank-you to your volunteers for donating their time (and often materials) to your space. An easy way to do this is to have kids make a giant thank-you card, take a photo of your group of kids holding it, and mail or email it to the volunteer. With my weekly volunteers I also purchase or make them a gift at the end of each semester.

If you have the budget to hire staff, even part-time, then you're already a step ahead. Take your time with this. It's much more important to hire someone who's a good fit for your culture than someone who already has all of the making skills. Finding someone with a willingness to learn; someone who's great with kids goes much farther than an expert who's grouchy or impatient. Consider asking them to prepare a making lesson as part of the interview process. Have them teach it to you or – even better – to some students.

## Materials Management

Another challenge to makerspace is managing all of the materials. There's no option that will allow you to keep everything neat and orderly all of the time. However, with a little planning you can keep it manageable. There are many effective ways to organize and distribute materials. We'll cover several in this section, but you may need to do some experimentation before you figure out what works best in your space. I tweak how everything is run and organized in my makerspace at least once a semester. You'll find that materials management is always ongoing.

### Labeled Tubs and Kits

Most makerspaces for kids have at least some of their materials organized into labeled tubs. If you have the funding to purchase differently sized, clear plastic tubs with lids, and a good label maker, I would strongly recommend doing so. Due to the limited funding in my makerspace, we have a mishmash of different types of storage containers. However, every container is clearly labeled, the shelves are labeled, and similar materials are grouped together. For example, all of the materials used for jewelry making – beads, wire, findings, floss – are all in labeled bins next to each other on adjacent shelves. We also have tubs with kits that contain all of the materials that you are likely to need to complete a particular project.

### Separating and Rotating Materials

I have two main spaces that students have access to, dubbed the "create space" and the "green screen room," and I have an office to store items that are adult-use only. In the "create space" I keep consumable materials that are inexpensive and unlimited use, such as magazines, yarn, beads, and cardboard. In the "green screen" room I keep materials that are limited. These are more expensive (less often donated) items such as coin batteries, copper tape, LEDs, and motors. I keep materials in my office that I feel are too dangerous for (5th and 6th grade) student use, but that I utilize to help them on a project, such as hand saws and box cutters.

We keep additional materials in the back (duct tape, Shrinky Dinks DIY plastic) that we rotate into the makerspace based on interest and need. We also put materials back into storage when students aren't utilizing them in the intended ways. We've had to do this with balloons and pillow fill, in the past.

I also have a tub on my desk with tools marked "Ask First." This is where I keep my Canary tools, tweezers, Sharpies, and other tools that tend to get lost, or that I want to more carefully monitor.

I have a large piece of cardboard on my desk labeled in Sharpie with the words "Hot Spot." This is where I have students leave the unplugged 3Doodler pens and hot glue guns when they're done using them. This way when the next group comes in, 5 minutes after the first group of makers has left, they will know to be cautious with these tools, to avoid getting burnt fingers.

Our makerspace is utilized by student-driven passion projects. This brings an extra challenge to management and organization because we can have as many as 31 students working on 31 different projects, simultaneously. I couldn't do this without my partner teachers. (I have one for my 5th grade elective classes and one for my 6th grade elective classes.) If you're managing a makerspace solo, it will run more smoothly if you have students work in groups, or if you have them all working on similar projects at once. When I teach passion projects solo, I require that students work in groups.

In other makerspaces, students work in groups to find a solution to a posed problem/essential question (project-based learning or PBL). Others still have students make at stations, where there are limited materials provided. You'll have to figure out what works best for you in your space.

### In-Progress and Finished Projects

You'll want to have a plan for where makers should store their in-progress projects. If you let them keep projects in your space, make sure they have a label (I use recycled index cards or sticky notes), with their name, the date, and a way to reach them in case they forget to come back for the project. If you work in a school, you might have them carry their materials to and from lockers. In my media center, we store projects on shelves in the back room and on the tops of the bookcases. It gets messy, but it's also cool to be able to see what everyone's working on.

When my makers finish their projects, they're required to put them in one of the display cases for a week, before they can bring them home. I ask them to include a label with their name, the date, and a description of the work, and a way to contact them if they forget to come back for their work. I model these after museum plaques. Having the kids' projects on display means that anyone who comes into the space can see some of the amazing projects they've made. It also helps give ideas to other kids, if they aren't sure what to make next. When my makers work really hard on something I also make a point to take photos of their work, and post them on social media.

# Trainings

Regardless of how your makerspace is organized, you'll need to provide training to students on using the tools. Particularly any tool that is hot, sharp, or complex. Since we have hundreds of kids using our makerspace every week, we can't monitor every project, and do every training at the whim of every student. Giving trainings takes time and attention away from attending to other students who may also need help, or just need more supervision. To effectively manage everything we have students write out their project plans before any trainings occur.

The trainings that we do are directly related to tools needed, as stated on the project plans. We then start with individual and group trainings. We will give group trainings for high-use tools such as 3Doodlers and hot glue guns. We give individual trainings to students who are using other tools, which are related to their project plans. Once we have trained a student, and they can effectively explain to us how to safely use the tool, they become a student mentor and can train other students on that specific tool. The newly trained student has to check in with us, and quickly tell us what they learned. If you wanted to, you could take a step further and have your makers create how-to videos. You could have your own channel, and have makers new to the project watch peer-created videos.

Before a student is allowed to use any hot or sharp tools, they're also required to read and sign a contract (a grownup at home has to sign it too). All of our makers wear lanyards when using the makerspace with their names, a stamp once they've returned the signed contract, and stamps for all training that they've completed. The makerspace contract is also provided on the following pages. Feel free to print or adapt this.

# Handout: Makerspace Student Safety Contract

Makerspace is very hands-on. You may be doing activities that require the use of hot or sharp objects. Safety in makerspace is the #1 priority for students, teachers, and parents/guardians. To ensure a safe space, students need to understand and follow these rules.

## General Rules

1. Always follow instructions carefully. If you don't understand something – ask!
2. Always grab your lanyard before you begin working.
3. Wait to touch tools/equipment until instructed to do so.
4. Only use tools that you have been trained to use safely.
5. Always use tools as they are intended to be used. For example, do not use a screwdriver as a hammer.
6. Think through your entire project before you start – figure out what you will need and how you will make it. Use the Project Planning sheet.
7. Report any accident or injury to teachers immediately – even something as small as a papercut.
8. Know where the Band-Aids and the first aid kit are. Know what other safety equipment we have and where it is located.
9. Always wear protective gear when needed; for example, safety goggles when taking things apart.
10. Always clean up any messes you make.
11. Make sure all equipment is unplugged and put away before leaving. If you use anything hot (hot glue gun, 3Doodler), leave it on the Hot Spot.
12. If you break a tool, replace it.
13. If you use any consumables, bring in something from home; see attached wish list for ideas of what to bring in.

## Makerspace Student Safety Promise

I, _____[write your first and last name], promise to follow the safety rules on this student safety contract, and all other instructions given to me by the makerspace teachers.

I promise to:

- Follow all safety rules given.
- Only use a tool when I have permission and have had training on how to use that tool.
- Immediately report all injuries or accidents.
- Make safe choices.
- Help other stay safe.
- Clean up after myself.

Continued participation in makerspace is dependent upon following these rules!

I have read and understand the Makerspace Student Safety Contract and Promise. I understand that not following the rules listed in these may result in my suspension from the Makerspace.

Student Signature:_____ Date: _____

Homeroom Teacher's Name_____

Makerspace Parent/Guardian Permission

Parent/Guardian Name (Please Print):_____

Parent/Guardian Email:_____

Parent/Guardian Phone:_____

Parent/Guardian Signature:_____ Date: _____

    In signing this document, I give my child permission to use all available makerspace tools and equipment.

## SOPs

SOPs (Standard Operating Procedures) are another good way to help kids use tools properly. These are step-by-step guides, commonly used in manufacturing, as well as professional makerspaces, to explain the steps and safety requirements for using tools and equipment. We try and keep our SOPs limited to one page, with images. This makes it more likely that the maker is actually going to use it. Consider laminating your SOPs and keeping them with the project materials or taping them to the table or the wall, if you have dedicated work stations.

## Environment and Inclusion

When you're deciding on maker activities in your space, it's important to make sure that different kinds of maker activities are included. If only certain activities are introduced, some of your kids may feel excluded or disinterested. I often see this in spaces that focus exclusively on technology, hand tools, and robotics, at the exclusion of crafting and more arts-focused making.

Also, representation matters. Be thoughtful about the examples you use throughout your makerspace. If you have images or posters displayed, make certain they're diverse. Try and have visual examples of makers who are male, female, and gender-neutral from backgrounds that represent the backgrounds of your kids, and backgrounds of people all over the world.

Makerspace should be a place where kids feel welcome, a space that kids get excited about. This won't happen if they feel excluded, or think the people who succeed in makerspace aren't people who look like them. Be cognizant of this.

## Conclusion

Managing an effective makerspace requires a lot of front-loaded planning and organization. You'll want to bring in volunteers, make sure that you support them, and run a background check before you have them working with kids. It will take some trial and error to figure out the best way to organize your space. This will also depend upon what your space looks like and the tools and materials that you're using. This will need to be tweaked and updated as your space gets used. It's a good idea to have kids and adults sign a contract or some sort of waiver before using hot or sharp objects. You may want to have a lawyer, administrator, or director sign off on your contract/waiver before engaging in makerspace activities.

# References

Plano Public Library. (2020). Library Make: Literacy Crafts & Tutorials. Retrieved February 16, 2021, from https://www.youtube.com/playlist?list=PLDDS7bPrXRJeQ1SGazyAVwaWteqeGp8IR

SEL: What Are the Core Competence Areas and Where are they Promoted? (2021). Retrieved February 16, 2021, from https://casel.org/sel-framework/

# Index

3D printing 46–7, 124–5, 127–8, 130
3Doodler 128, 134, 136–7

Adobe Spark 40
Anchor 84
Arduino 124, 128
Audacity 84

barter system 120, 123–5, 131
borrowing materials 120, 123–5, 131
brainstorming 3, 7, 15, 40–1, 45, 47, 99, 103–6
bristlebots 124
button making: design handout 41; project 39–45

Canary tools 8, 11, 14, 21, 134
card making: guidelines for writing cards handout 33; project 27–33 see also paper circuits
cardboard challenge: hosting reproducible 22; project 18–25; reflection handout 25
CASEL's SEL Framework: Relationship Skills 13, 15, 18–20, 26–8, 30, 34, 36, 38–9, 45, 47, 51, 54, 58, 62–5, 70–1, 79, 84, 98, 103–4, 106, 109, 111–2, 114, 118; Responsible Decision-Making 1–3, 5, 7, 13–5, 17–9, 26, 28, 30, 34–5, 38–9, 46–7, 51–2, 54, 58, 63, 70–1, 79, 84, 92, 98, 103, 106, 109, 111, 113–5; Self-Awareness 13, 18–9, 24, 26, 28, 34, 36, 39, 46, 62–4, 70–1, 75, 79–80, 85, 98, 100, 102, 104, 106, 109, 112, 114–5, 118–9; Self-Management 1–2, 5, 7, 13–5, 18–9, 23, 26, 28, 30, 34–6, 39, 45–6, 51, 54, 58, 60, 63, 71, 79, 84, 98, 106, 112, 115, 118; Social Awareness 1, 13–4, 19–20, 23, 26, 28, 32, 34–5, 38–9, 45, 47, 51, 54, 58, 61–3, 65, 71, 79–80, 84, 98, 102–3, 106, 109, 111–2
chroma key 71–2 see also green screen
Chromebook 63–4, 69, 89

citations 89, 93–4
CNC router 130
creative commons licensing 123, 131

Dic CC Mixter 85, 92
deckle 28, 30–1
donations: 19–20, 22, 26, 53, 61, 120–2, 125, 127, 131

empathy 13, 19, 26, 28, 32, 34, 58, 61

fabric pen 51–2, 54, 58–9
fair use 72
Flipgrid 64, 70
fleece 50–1, 54, 56–9, 61
free: consumables 120–1, 124, 131; digital resources 123; for educational use 123 see also fair use
fundraising: book fairs 125–7, 131; crowd-funding 125, 127, 131; Foundation Directory Online 128–9; GrantSpace 129; Grant Watch 129; grant writing 125, 128–9; Maker Faire 127, 131

G. Suite: Drive 64, 85, 95; Slides 84–5, 90, 93, 96
Genius Hour 115, 119
giant dice 12–18
Google see G: Suite
grant writing see fundraising
green screen 62, 64, 69, 71–8, 98, 134

hot glue/guns 46–7, 121, 134

iMovie 72–8 see also green screen
inclusion 18, 27, 47, 139
inclusive playground: design handout 48; project 45–9
infinity scarf 53–7

K'nex 46

Lanyards 115, 118, 136–7
laser cutters/engravers 46, 130
LittleBits 126, 128

Make Beliefs Comix 67
makerspace: donations policy reproducible 121; general safety rules handout 4; student safety contract 137–138; student makers as mentors 118; student trainings 135–6
Makedo tools 8–11, 14, 20–1
Makey Makey 126, 128
materials management: labeling 134; rotating 134–5; project storage 135

no-sew scarf 50–3
no-sew tie pillow 57–61

open source: 84, 123, 131
Ozobot 21

pair and share 5, 48
paper circuits 34–9 *see also* card making
passion projects: anticipating obstacles 111; assigning roles 111–2; brainstorming handout 105; independent planning form handout 117; my favorite things handout 101; planning and feedback handout 108; rubric handout 110
podcasting: note taking handout 81; project 79–84; script guidelines handout 83
podcasts for kids 80
Poll Everywhere 45
presentations: delivery 113–5; design 113
project-based learning 135
prototype 23, 27, 45–8, 110, 112, 114, 125

quilter's ruler 51–2, 54, 58–9

safety rules 1–4, 14, 137
Screencastify 64
SeeSaw 24, 70
Skil power screwdriver/cutter tool 8, 12–5
slideshow design *see* presentations
smart phone 64, 69
snowball microphone 69
SOPs 139
sound transmission loss/STL 69
stabilizer rig 69
Stop-Breath-Look and Think 2, 5–6
storyboard/storyboarding 62–4, 67, 69, 110
soundproofing *see* sound transmission loss
Swivl 69

Tinkercad 47

Unity 123
Universal Design 45, 47, 49
unsafe choices: act it out 7; make a plan 3
Unsplash 72, 85, 88
upcycling *see* recycling

video: movie storyboard handout 68; recording 69; script starter handout 66; sharing 70; transferring 69–70
virtual calming room 84–98
Vocaroo 84
volunteers 23, 126, 132–3, 139

WeVideo 64
word cloud 45

Zoom 64, 71

For Product Safety Concerns and Information please contact our EU
representative  GPSR@taylorandfrancis.com
Taylor & Francis Verlag GmbH, Kaufingerstraße 24, 80331 München, Germany

www.ingramcontent.com/pod-product-compliance
Lightning Source LLC
Chambersburg PA
CBHW081827230426
43668CB00017B/2399